D0873920

Medical Interpreting and Cross-cultural Communication

When healthcare providers and patients do not speak the same language, medical interpreters are called in to help. In this book – the first ever ethnographic study of a bilingual hospital – Claudia V. Angelelli explores the role of medical interpreters, drawing on data from over 300 medical encounters and interviewing the interpreters themselves about the people for whom they interpret, their challenges, and how they characterize their role. Traditionally the interpreter has been viewed as a language conduit, with little power over the medical encounter or the relationship between patient and provider. This book presents an alternative view, considering the interpreter's agency and contextualizing the practice within an institution that is part of a larger society. Bringing together literature from social theory, social psychology, and linguistic anthropology, this book will be welcomed by anyone who wants to discover the intricacies of medical interpreting firsthand; particularly researchers, communication specialists, policy makers, and practitioners.

CLAUDIA V. ANGELELLI is Associate Professor of Spanish Linguistics at San Diego State University, where she teaches applied linguistics courses such as Spanish discourse analysis, English–Spanish translation and interpreting theory, and methods of teaching Spanish. Her research focuses on cross-linguistic and cross-cultural communication, and she has published articles in a variety of journals, such as *The Annual Review of Applied Linguistics*, *META: Journal des Traducteurs* and *Critical Link: Interpreters in the Community*.

Medical Interpreting and Cross-cultural Communication

Claudia V. Angelelli

San Diego State University

CAMBRIDGE
UNIVERSITY PRESS

PUBLISHED BY THE PRESS SYNDICATE OF THE UNIVERSITY OF CAMBRIDGE
The Pitt Building, Trumpington Street, Cambridge, United Kingdom

CAMBRIDGE UNIVERSITY PRESS
The Edinburgh Building, Cambridge CB2 2RU, UK
40 West 20th Street, New York, NY 10011–4211, USA
477 Williamstown Road, Port Melbourne, VIC 3207, Australia
Ruiz de Alarcón 13, 28014 Madrid, Spain
Dock House, The Waterfront, Cape Town 8001, South Africa

http://www.cambridge.org

First published 2004

Printed in the United Kingdom at the University Press, Cambridge

Typefaces Times 10/12 pt.   *System* LATEX 2$_\varepsilon$ [TB]

A catalogue record for this book is available from the British Library

Library of Congress Cataloguing in Publication data
Angelelli, Claudia (Claudia V.)
Medical interpreting and cross-cultural communication / Claudia Angelelli.
     p.   cm.
Includes bibliographical references and index.
ISBN 0 521 83026 5
1. Medicine – Translating.   2. Intercultural communication.   3. Translating services –
California – Case studies.   4. Hispanic Americans – Services for – California – Case studies.
5. Hispanic Americans – Hospital care – California – Case studies.   I. Title.
R119.5.A53   2004
610′.1′4 – dc22   2004045688

ISBN 0 521 83026 5 hardback

To my mother, Angela Rizzo, whose dedication to science and public health served as an inspiration

To my husband, Christian Degueldre, whose longtime interest and work in this topic and incredible support helped make this work a reality

Contents

List of figures   *page* ix
List of tables   x
Acknowledgments   xi
List of abbreviations   xiii

Prologue   1

1 Questioning invisibility   7
   Previous studies on interpreting in a medical setting   12

2 Communication in the medical encounter   15
   The essence of the doctor–patient relationship   15
   Communication issues in a bilingual medical encounter   18
   Navigating across languages and cultures: the need for
      interpreters   21

3 A different set of lenses   26
   Looking at the interpreter's role through different lenses   26
      The lens of society and the institution   27
      The lens of the interaction   29
      The lens of discourse   33
   Monolingual and interpreted communicative events:
      differences and similarities   34

4 California Hope: a public hospital in changing times   44
   Finding a study site   44
   The pilot study   44
   Obtaining consent   45
   The in-depth study   46
      The town   46
      The hospital   46
      The study site   48
      The staff   48
      The workplace   52
      Working hours and interpreters' responsibilities   53
      A typical day at Interpreting Services   55

5   Putting it all together   58
      Data collection, coding, and analysis   59
        Artifacts   59
        Field notes   59
        The interpreter interpersonal role inventory   61
        Interviews   62
        Audio recordings of ICEs   63
      Categories and subcategories emerging from ICEs   69
        Nature of the ICE   69
        Intention of the ICE   70
        Visibility of the interpreter   71

6   Finding visibility   73
      The nature of the ICE at California Hope   73
      The structure of the ICE at California Hope   74
      Interpreter visibility: an overview   75
      Manifestations of visibility in ICEs at California Hope   76
      Becoming visible: linguistic and communicative strategies   77
      Minor visibility: occasional involvement of interpreter as co-owner
        of text   79
        Typical openings of an ICE   79
        Typical closings of an ICE   82
      Major visibility: interpreters as owners of text   85

7   Interpreters' voices   105
      Roberto, the manager   105
      Annette   108
      Consuelo   110
      Elda   112
      Joaquín   114
      Julio   118
      Marcos   120
      Mariana   121
      Mauro   123
      Rogelio   124
      Vicente   125

8   Emerging metaphors and final words   129
      Interpreters as detectives   129
      Interpreters as multi-purpose bridges   130
      Interpreters as diamond connoisseurs   131
      Interpreters as miners   131
      Pulling it all together   132
        Theoretical implications   133
        Practical implications   135
      Concerns and curiosities revisited   140

    References   142
    Index   147

Figures

1 The invisible interpreter   *page* 8
2 The interpreter as co-constructor   8
3 The visible interpreter   10
4 Multiple lenses to look at the interpreter in an ICE   27
5 Interpreting service floor plan   54
6 Examples of an index entry of an ICE   66
7 Example of visibility in an index entry   70
8 The visibility continuum at California Hope   78

Tables

1 Fundamental notions of monolingual and interpreted
  communicative events   *page* 35
2 California Hope interpreters' demographic data   50
3 Artifacts   60
4 Field notes   60
5 Interpreter interpersonal role inventory (IPRI)   62
6 Interviews   62
7 Audio recordings of interpreted communicative events (ICEs)   65
8 Inventory of ICEs   68

Acknowledgments

This book would not have been possible without the help and kindness of the California Hope community. Over a period of twenty-two months, patients and their family members, healthcare providers, interpreters, and other employees at California Hope allowed me to intrude in their lives and work, even at personal and delicate moments. To them goes my greatest acknowledgment of gratitude. They cannot be mentioned by name, but they all know who they are, and they will recognize their contributions to this book.

This book evolves from thoughts and perspectives which I first presented in my PhD thesis on an interdisciplinary approach to the role of interpreters across settings (Angelelli 2001). A special acknowledgment goes to Dr. Guadalupe Valdés who has been a source of inspiration through both her scholarly work and her commitment to social justice, especially for the Latino population. She provided confidence and guidance throughout my work at California Hope. I am also grateful to Dr. Shirley Brice-Heath for introducing me to the scholarly study of ethnography of communication, which I applied to medical interpreting. She has been a model for me as a scholar, researcher, and writer. I am indebted to Dr. Ray McDermott for the extended discussions on analysis of social interaction which showed me how to step beyond the boundaries. I also try to follow his steps as a scholar and analyst. I am grateful to Dr. Edward Haertel who crossed disciplinary boundaries to offer critical support as well as insight into the research product and process. Although I am ultimately responsible for the final product, these individuals have had a positive impact on the development of this work, and I am forever indebted to them.

Janice Kezirian, MD, is behind this book more than any other single individual. Her scientific knowledge and integrity are evident throughout. Her theoretical approach to the study of doctor–patient communication, coupled with her experiences as a physician in Mexico and her commitment on a personal level to making communication and language relevant to medical practice, have influenced nearly every interpretation of this book. Her enthusiasm, support, and patience for my work have been *very* important. Her sense of humor and friendship are gifts I treasure.

Special recognition goes to my husband, Christian Degueldre, an outstanding interpreter, translator and interpreting professor, and loving human being. His professional recognition in the field of interpreting paved my way into California Hope. During the data collection period, he was extremely patient with the repeated tales about each day I spent at the site. He has encouraged me in the completion of this book, and he has been most helpful in verifying data and references, as well as in offering insightful comments on multiple readings of the draft.

I am also grateful to Dr. Cynthia Roy for invaluable comments on sections of this book. Her insights and challenges have strengthened my arguments. Additionally I would like to thank Dr. Katherina Brett, Helen Barton, Kay McKechnie, and Dr. Alison Powell of Cambridge University Press for their guidance in the preparation of this book for publication. My hope is that this work and the findings reported here will be of benefit to those concerned with issues of healthcare, and that it will help them promote fair and culturally sensitive communicative environments for speakers of minority languages.

Abbreviations

ASL   American Sign Language
CH   California Hope
D   doctor
EMT   emergency medical technician
HCP   healthcare provider
HI   hospital interpreter
ICE   interpreted communicative event
IPRI   Interpreter interpersonal role inventory
IS   interpreting services
MAC   medical admitting clerk
MCE   monolingual communicative event
N   nurse
P   patient
SES   socio-economic status

Prologue

The end of the twentieth century and the beginning of the twenty-first witnessed important changes affecting healthcare delivery to limited-English-speaking patients in the United States. As a result, a gradual emergence of academic questions regarding the nature of communication between healthcare providers and patients across gulfs of language and culture, especially when brokered by interpreters, began to trigger debate as to what roles the interpreters should play. This concern was echoed in practical pleas of interpreters themselves who asked: "What can I do to help, what is my role?"

The field of medical interpreting, in particular, has been undergoing an extraordinary evolution. First, Title VI of the Civil Rights Act of 1964 established the need for professional interpreters, in order to ensure meaningful access to healthcare for patients with limited English proficiency. As a result, government-funded programs for healthcare institutions have been mandated to provide interpreting services to limited-English-speaking patients (Allen 2000). At the same time, medical interpreter organizations are writing and publishing codes of ethics and pursuing certification efforts (California Healthcare Interpreters Association 2002; Massachusetts Medical Interpreters Association 1995). Funding agencies are increasingly paying attention to issues of cross-cultural and linguistic communication. In 2001, the Robert Wood Johnson Foundation funded *Hablamos Juntos*, an 18-million-dollar national initiative to improve healthcare communication for the Latino population in the United States. At the time this book was written, Latinos were the largest and fastest growing racial/ethnic group in the United States with 35.33 million, 12.5 percent of the total population, counted in the 2000 census (US Bureau of Census, May 2000).

Finally, legislation banning the use of children as interpreters in healthcare institutions (Yee, Diaz, and Spitzer 2003) and publications denouncing the use of bilingual janitors and untrained interpreters (Allen 2000; Cambridge 1999; Marcus 2003) have been fueling the debate on the quality of access to healthcare available to speakers of non-societal languages in a multilingual society.

The challenging times in which we live have also witnessed changes in the perception of medical interpreting as a profession, and the role of medical

1

interpreters. Up until the 1990s, medical interpreting was perceived as a less prestigious variety of interpreting, practiced mostly by *ad hoc* interpreters. Without a theoretical underpinning to account for the special type of interaction that occurs in a medical setting, medical interpreting standards of practice and ethical principles have been largely based on conference or court practices. In many cases, these standards and principles have been blindly transferred to the medical setting, and in a few cases they have been adapted to address the complexities of medical interpreting to a limited extent. Central to the standards of practice has been the role of the interpreter.

Throughout these changing times, I have donned various hats within the field of translation and interpreting: a researcher concerned with equal access to communication and services on the part of limited-English patients and with the different roles that interpreters play; a teacher of translation and interpreting; and an active member of various professional associations engaged in writing a code of ethics and designing assessment instruments to measure interpreters' performances. As a result of these experiences, I have observed and interacted with many interpreters. Through their words and actions, I have witnessed the emergence of a tension, which has become a source of interest for me. It seems that a contradiction exists between the role that is prescribed for interpreters (through codes and rules, both inside and outside the classrooms) and the role that unfolds in the practice of interpreting (in hospitals, in meetings, in the courts, at schools, and in the community at large). Schools and associations prescribe an invisible interpreter. However, the interpreter at work seems very visible to me.

Concerns and curiosities

The dilemma between the prescribed role of the interpreter and the reality of the interpreter at work sparked a concern and a curiosity within me. The concern is at the level of both theory and practice. I find it problematic that an entire field could be rooted in what seems like a myth (Metzger 1999): that interpreters can be neutral or invisible, and that invisibility is in fact plausible and presented as an ideal. At the theoretical level, if the knowledge base of interpreting seems to lie in the myth of an invisible interpreter, then what are the underlying assumptions of this myth, and what are the reasons for its existence? What does it mean for an interpreter to be invisible? How can an interpreter be invisible? In fact, how can any interlocutor in any instance of communication be invisible? Do related theories exist that would support the invisibility myth? Can the field of interpreting continue to hold to the belief system of invisibility when the very nature of interpreting intersects with other fields (such as intercultural communication, interpersonal relations, social psychology, bilingualism, sociolinguistics, and cultural anthropology), which have suggested that invisibility is not plausible? What ideology underlies the blocking of the self, placing it in a social vacuum, and believing that this is plausible? What underlies the perpetuation of such ideology? A field cannot advance without an underlying theory. An underlying theory that is based on a myth is not a substantial theory. This is a genuine concern.

At the level of practice, my concern is about the ways in which the belief system of invisibility impacts on the lives of those who rely on interpreters for their daily communicative needs (who are some of the most vulnerable members of society) as well as the interpreters themselves and the healthcare providers (HCPs). For speakers of non-societal languages, access to service and information depends entirely on interpreters. These interpreters are powerful parties in helping speakers of minority languages accomplish their communicative goals. I am also curious about how interpreters ground their practice in the unchallenged belief of invisibility. What does it mean to be a bridge between more and less dominant cultures? What responsibility does it entail? How much responsibility should interpreters be willing to accept? Do they need to accept the mandate imposed on them by society or by their professional associations, or can they alter it? What role do they want to play? Do they exercise the agency they have, and if so, how? Under the guise of invisibility, practitioners, teachers of interpreting, and professional associations are turning a deaf ear toward these issues. This is another genuine concern.

These concerns and curiosities compelled me to problematize the dilemma of the invisible interpreter, and explore the role of the visible interpreter. For that exploration, I needed a home.

Looking for a home: interpreting and the ethnography of communication

The study of medical interpreting should occur in a natural setting and for a prolonged period of time. Thorough studies in discourse analysis and interpreting (e.g. Davidson 2000; Metzger 1999; Roy 2000; Wadensjö 1998) have begun to challenge the notion of neutrality and invisibility present in the prescribed role of interpreters. However, I wanted to expand on their work by studying a larger number of interactions. What I discovered was that studying interpreted medical discourse for an extended period of time is as revealing as it is complex. It allows the exploration of issues that can only be addressed through time.

That is why between June 1999 and April 2001, I followed, observed, and worked with a team of medical interpreters in a Northern California hospital. My goal in studying medical interpreting at this hospital, which I call California

Hope, was exploratory. Guided by my concern and my curiosity about how medical interpreters work, I took an ethnographic approach to the role of the interpreter (entering without a hypothesis). At the time I did this study, models within the field of medical interpreting were not available (cf. Berk-Seligson 1990 for a study of a bilingual courtroom); it was the first ethnography to be carried out in a bilingual medical setting. Conducting an ethnography meant being present to observe, record, and write down what was seen and heard, and ask what on the surface seemed like over-simplistic questions, but questions which turned out to be important ones indeed. It also required cross-checking, comparing, and triangulating the information obtained before it became the solid foundation on which to build my knowledge base.

Like all ethnographers, I experienced periods of feeling overwhelmed by the volume of my data, and times when I could not bear to think about ending the process of data collection. Leaving the fieldwork was not easy; leaving the people was even more difficult. After all the shared experiences, I felt as much part of their lives as they had become of mine. Although I very much wanted to continue working in the hospital and being part of California Hope, I also felt compelled to work toward addressing the concern and curiosity that had brought me to California Hope in the first place. Being an ethnographer means leaving the study site and responsibly telling its story. That is what this book is about.

Plan of the book

Chapter 1 opens up a discussion of the interpreter's role during a cross-linguistic encounter. It shows how different paradigms have portrayed the role of the interpreter and offers a model that encompasses the challenges faced by professionals of goodwill.

Chapter 2 explores the interaction between patient and healthcare provider. It discusses the importance of establishing a positive relationship in different settings: where both patient and healthcare provider share the same language and cultural background; where they communicate through a shared language but they do not have a common cultural background; and where patient and provider share neither language nor culture and must communicate through an interpreter.

In chapter 3, I present a new set of lenses (the intersection of social psychology, social theory, and linguistic anthropology) that allows for a broader discussion on the role of the interpreter. By considering the interpreter's role as a specific type of interpersonal relation and contextualizing it within an institution that is part of a larger society, social factors are highlighted. The role that the interpreter plays in bridging major gulfs of class, culture, and education becomes evident.

Chapter 4 introduces the reader to California Hope. It describes the process of building trust and gaining entry, and the reasons for choosing California Hope as the site for this study. It also provides a detailed description of the participants, the interpreting service for which they work, their physical workspace, and their daily routine.

Chapter 5 outlines the data collected in this study (artifacts, audio recordings of medical appointments, field notes, interviews, and questionnaires) and the processes used for coding and analyses.

In chapter 6, I examine the materialization of the role of interpreters at California Hope. I present and analyze segments of interpreted communicative events at the hospital, both face-to-face and over the speakerphone. Various segments illustrate typical behaviors of interpreters at work, demonstrating different degrees of interpreters' visibility during the interactions.

Chapter 7 portrays how medical interpreters talk about their work, the people for whom they interpret, the challenges and stressful moments they must overcome, and how they characterize their role.

Chapter 8 reveals a series of metaphors that interpreters use when they talk about their jobs. These metaphors reflect the underlying tension between their beliefs about their role and their accounts of what they actually do when they interpret. This chapter revisits the concern and the curiosity about the interpreter's role and offers discussion and conclusions from the analysis performed. It also addresses the theoretical and practical implications of the study.

This book was written to appeal to a variety of readers, such as researchers, policy makers, interpreter–educators, practitioners, students of interpreting, healthcare professionals, and communication specialists. Researchers concerned with interpreting as a specific event of cross-cultural communication may make the most use of the citations that place this book at the intersection of social psychology, sociology, and linguistic anthropology. Policy makers and researchers involved in issues of healthcare access for linguistic minorities may find it interesting to study interpreting as it interacts with cross-cultural communication. Interpreters and interpreter–educators will find insights about a practice that, although portrayed as simple and straightforward, is rich and complex. Professional associations of interpreters may benefit from discussions in this book as they continue a dialogue on education and certification in this field. Healthcare professionals may gain an awareness of some of the challenges and advantages of communicating through an interpreter. Any interested reader will have a chance to discover the intricacies of medical interpreting firsthand. The descriptions and analyses in the body of the book will raise numerous questions for these readers. My hope is that their questions will be directed not only to the contents of this book, but also toward theories and generalizations from their own disciplines about how people communicate in a healthcare encounter.

I have made every effort possible to conceal the real names of people and places in this book. All names are pseudonyms and all figures are rounded up to ensure confidentiality. During my work at California Hope, I intruded in the lives of many people, most of whom were patients during some of their weakest and most vulnerable moments. I took the responsibility for the influence of my presence, my ideas, and my role as a participant observer. My intention is to take the same responsibility in writing this book.

1   Questioning invisibility

Science would be superfluous if the outward appearance and the essence of things directly coincided.

Karl Marx, *Capital*, vol. 3, part VII, ch. 48, p.iii

Communication between speakers who do not share a common language or culture has always been enabled by translation or interpreting. Interpreters are one component in a three-factor equation, which consists of more-dominant speakers, less-dominant speakers, and the interpreter. The role of interpreters in a bilingual encounter can take different forms. For example interpreters may help minority-language speakers explore possibilities, thereby channeling opportunities for them. This brokering may be achieved by being attentive to the social reality of the speakers. Alternatively, interpreters may focus on the message only, disregarding how it is socially constructed by each of the parties involved in the conversation. Another possibility is that interpreters may align with the speaker of the societal language, conveying information to the less-dominant speakers without helping them gain access to it. This last possibility positions interpreters as gatekeepers (Davidson 2001) rather than opportunity channels. Regardless of the role assumed by interpreters in the cross-linguistic encounter, they are vital for the communication of those who do not speak the majority language.

Language interpreters are often portrayed as *invisible* language facilitators. According to this perception of invisibility, interpreters are not considered to be parties to the conversation, but rather they are seen as language-switching operators in line with the conduit model of communication (Reddy 1979). As such, interpreters are expected to pay close attention to the meaning of the message expressed by the parties to a conversation and to convey that same meaning into the other language, without omissions or additions. This perception of invisibility is represented as a model in figure 1. Based on conference interpreting, this belief supports the idea that only one meaning exists for each verbal utterance and that this meaning is not subject to co-construction. Thus, there exists only one possible rendition for that meaning. This conceptualization of interpreting considers accuracy over all other aspects that can be attributed to the

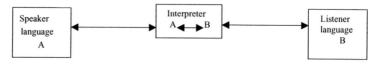

Figure 1   The invisible interpreter (adapted from AIIC 2002; Seleskovitch and Lederer 1989; and Weber 1984)

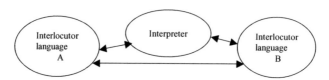

Figure 2   The interpreter as a co-constructor (adapted from Berk-Seligson 1990; Metzger 1999; Roy 2000; and Wadensjö 1998)

message (e.g. intention of the parties, goal of the communicative event, or context of the interaction). The concept of invisibility presumes: (1) no interaction between interpreters and speakers (by limiting the interpreters' participation to language switching); (2) no interaction between speakers themselves (e.g. body language); and (3) interpreting can occur in a social vacuum since it overlooks social and cultural factors brought to the interaction by the interpreters and the two speakers.

An alternative conceptualization of the role of interpreters is represented in figure 2. In this view, interpreters are seen as essential partners, or in other words, *co-constructors* to the interaction (Berk-Seligson 1990; Metzger 1999; Roy 1989, 2000; Wadensjö 1992, 1995, and 1998). Interpreters' participation is evidenced by constructing, co-constructing, repairing, and facilitating the talk. This approach to interpreting as interaction shifts the conceptualization of mechanical or invisible interpreters to more active co-participants.

Research in sociolinguistics emphasizes crucial differences in the participatory role of interpreters, and these differences depend upon the nature of the interpreted communicative event (ICE) (Hymes 1974). The interpreter as a co-participant to the ICE has been studied extensively using discourse analysis (Davidson 1998, 2000, 2001; Metzger 1999; Roy 1989, 2000; Wadensjö 1995, 1998). Davidson (2000, 2001) and Metzger (1999) challenge the notion of neutrality, while studying the participation of interpreters during interactions. Roy (2000) discusses interpreting as a special case of discourse process. She performs a deep analysis of a conference between a professor and a (deaf) student mediated by an American Sign Language–English interpreter, and shows the active participation of the interpreter in the interaction. By using Goffman's framework of roles (1981), she addresses "the shifts interpreters make from relaying messages to managing and coordinating talk" (2000: 111). Roy's analysis specifically looks at two instances where a participant addresses the interpreter directly, and the interpreter speaks back to this participant. The role is analyzed in terms of "responsibility for the flow and maintenance of communication" by focusing on turn taking (2000: 121). Like Metzger and Roy, Wadensjö (1998) uses Goffman's framework of roles to question the normative character of the literature in interpreting that characterizes how interpreters "should perform" instead of looking at the performances of interpreters in actual cases (1998: 83).

These scholars call for further research to study the role of interpreters as co-participants in the interaction. They also underscore the fact that interpreting does not happen in a social vacuum and the importance of describing the role of interpreters in the social context where the interaction is embedded. This book begins to address this call by investigating the *visible* role of interpreters as it materializes in a medical setting.

The concept of visible interpreters goes beyond the fact that they are active participants in the linguistic interaction. It takes into consideration the power that interpreters possess. The model of visibility that I propose portrays interpreters who are not only linguistically visible, but who are also visible with all the social and cultural factors that allow them to co-construct a definition of reality with the other co-participants to the interaction. Interpreters enter the interaction with all of their deeply held views on power, status, solidarity, gender, age, race, ethnicity, nationality, socio-economic status (SES), as well as the cultural norms and societal blueprints that encompass the encounter; they use all of these to construct and interpret reality. The interpreters' views of all of these social factors interact with the parties' views of those same social factors. Interpreters, as members of society, do more than merely co-construct and interact in the communicative event. They are powerful parties who are capable of altering the outcome of the interaction, for example, by channeling opportunities or facilitating access to information. They are visible co-participants who possess agency.

This visible model is highly complex because of several factors present in interpreting situations. Firstly, the ICE does not happen in a social vacuum. It occurs within one institution that is permeable to the mandates of society. As a consequence, various layers of institutional and societal influences surround the ICE, adding to its complexity. Secondly, each party to the ICE brings to the encounter its own social factors (race, ethnicity, age, gender, SES), adding to the complexity of the interaction. Finally, the very nature of interpreting is a highly sophisticated process that involves the juggling of these social factors,

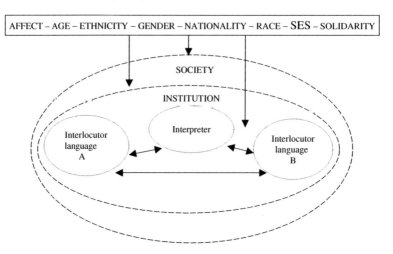

Figure 3   The visible interpreter (Angelelli 2001)

plus the information processing between languages and cultures, performed under pressure.

Figure 3 represents the complex role of the visible interpreter. The upper box represents cultural norms and blueprints. The outer circle shows how society enacts them. The middle circle represents the effect and re-creation of those cultural norms and blueprints within the institution. Within this circle lies another set of institutional norms and blueprints which get reconstructed and funneled to permeate the interactions that occur within its boundaries. In the inner circle, the interlocutors bring to the interaction their own set of beliefs, attitudes, and deeply held views on interpersonal factors, such as gender, race, ethnicity, and SES. During the ICE, the interpreter is also present with his/her own set of beliefs and deeply held views that are constructed, co-constructed, and reenacted within the interaction. As the ICE unfolds, the interpreter brings not only the knowledge of languages and the ability to language switch or assign turns, but also the self. Through the self, the interpreter exercises agency and power, which materialize through different behaviors that alter the outcome of the interaction. Interpreters are opaque rather than transparent, or visible rather than invisible.

The model on which this book is based builds on previous work by Berk-Seligson (1990), Davidson (1998), Metzger (1999), Prince (1986), Roy (1989, 2000), and Wadensjö (1998). It takes the following critical perspective: interpreters, as members of speech communities (Hymes 1974) in which there are asymmetrical relations between speakers of more and less dominant groups, possess deeply held views about power and solidarity (Davidson 2000, 2001).

Like any other human beings, interpreters also possess deeply held views regarding social factors, all of which are present as they interpret and interact during speech events (Brewer 1988; Festinger 1954; Stouffer et al. 1949).

The visible model presents interpreters who are capable of actively and consciously managing those issues as the interpretation unfolds. In practice, this is observed in varying degrees. The interpreters' role expands beyond that of transparent language modem to opaque co-participant. This model posits interpreters who make use not just of interpersonal and sociopolitical skills but also of the linguistic and psycholinguistic skills portrayed by the literature on interpreting.

Visibility and participation are not just present in the linguistic co-construction of the conversation, they are also essential in:
• communicating cultural gaps as well as linguistic barriers
• communicating affect nuances as well as the content of the message
• establishing trust between all parties to the conversation
• facilitating mutual respect
• putting the parties at ease during the conversation
• creating more balance (or imbalance) during the conversation (by aligning with one of the parties)
• advocating for or establishing alliances with either party
• managing the requested and given information

Visibility manifests itself when interpreters do one or more of the following: (1) introduce or position the self as a party to the ICE, thus becoming co-participants (Metzger 1999; Roy 2000; Wadensjö 1998) and co-constructors (Davidson 1998, 2000, 2001); (2) set communication rules (for example, turn-taking) and control the traffic of information (Roy 2000); (3) paraphrase or explain terms or concepts (Davidson 1998, 2000); (4) slide the message up and down the register scale (Angelelli 2001); (5) filter information (Davidson 1998, 2000); (6) align with one of the parties (Wadensjö 1998); and (7) replace one of the parties to the ICE (Roy 2000).

The interpreters on the opposite extreme of this continuum are individuals who repeat information in a different language and are not necessarily concerned with the parties' understanding or co-construction of the message. They follow the traffic flow (instead of controlling it) and ignore differences in register. This kind of interpreter is indifferent to the parties' access to the message or lack thereof, and is not active in the cross-cultural brokerage, but instead works with the message at the linguistic level only.

Taking an ethnographic approach to studying the role of the medical interpreter, I followed ten interpreters during a period of twenty-two months, and collected data from 392 ICEs. For these data to be meaningful, it is important to first consider the current literature on interpreting in a medical setting.

Previous studies on interpreting in a medical setting

Medical discourse and the role of the interpreter have been the subject of various studies (Bolden 2000; Cambridge 1999; Davidson 1998, 2000, 2001; Kaufert and Putsch 1997; Metzger 1999; Prince 1986; Shuy 1976; Wadensjö 1998).

On cross-linguistic communication, Bolden (2000) analyzes two interviews between English-speaking doctors and Russian-speaking patients. She examines the role of medical interpreters in structuring interaction between patients and providers in the history-taking phase of medical consultations. Bolden challenges the image of interpreters as non-participants to the interaction, whose role is limited to language conversion, and demonstrates that they orient toward obtaining medically relevant information from patients and conveying that information to providers. Focusing on a different linguistic group, Cambridge (1999) analyzes seven extempore simulated consultations between general medical practitioners and Spanish-speaking volunteer patients. Interpreting was provided by native speakers of Spanish who were not trained, professional interpreters. The results show that appropriate interlocutor roles are not always occupied by all parties and that dangers exist due to a lack of common ground within the transaction.

In a similar setting and with the same language pair, Davidson (1998) investigates medical discourse mediated by an interpreter. He examines the construction of reciprocity and meaning in interpreted conversations and offers a model which he then applies to ten interpreted and ten same-language medical interviews collected from a pool of fifty. Davidson concludes that the difficulties in interpreted conversations lie in the construction of reciprocal understanding as well as in the accurate transformation of semantic and pragmatic content, and that the role of the interpreter as linguistic facilitator varies according to the parties to the interaction. For the physician, the interpreter is the instrument that keeps the patient on track. For the patient, the interpreter is a co-conversationalist. In later work, Davidson (2000) also argues for the need to consider the context within which interpreters work and to analyze interpreters' actions against the historical and institutional context. He states that interpreters do not act merely as machines of semantic conversion, but rather as active participants in the diagnostic process, aligning with healthcare providers, and thus acting as gatekeepers (2001) for the recent immigrants for whom they interpret.

In a similar cross-linguistic environment, Prince (1986) investigates conversations between doctors and patients, using the question as the unit of analysis. She reports an asymmetric distribution in the number of questions asked and answered during a doctor–patient interview. Doctors asked the vast majority of information-seeking questions. Interpreters only initiated one percent of the questions. Three interpreter-related distortions identified in the discourse were: (1) answering instead of translating questions (generally occurring in the patient-substitute model); (2) incomplete translations (generally occurring in multiple-part questions); and (3) incorrect translations (sometimes related to the level of technicality of the term used or to the lower language proficiency of either the doctor or the interpreter, mishearing, and failure to check information). The elicitation of information through the use of questions is of utmost importance in the medical interview. However, as stated by Shuy (1976), this elicitation generally presents various problems triggered by differences in linguistic and cultural backgrounds as well as their goals and understanding of the interaction.

Kaufert and Putsch (1997) look at the dilemmas faced by medical personnel when two cultural systems clash in emergency situations. Their study considers day-to-day workplace pressures and ethical dilemmas, focusing on informed consent and end-of-life decisions mediated by interpreters. The cases used were part of a larger ethnographic study on the role of Aboriginal health interpreters in Winnipeg, Canada. Observations from healthcare providers in Seattle were also included. The discussion centers on issues of power and dominance in clinical communication, the challenge of monolingualism in multicultural medical practice and the role of language intermediaries (interpreters). The authors object to the role of neutrality prescribed for interpreters by the code of ethics of certain interpreter organizations and argue for ethics that would address instances when interpreters "act as advocates for patients" (p. 77). The authors state that "healthcare interpretation often occurs across major gulfs of culture, class and language, and therefore it is unlike interpretation in the courts or in business or international negotiation. Attempts to encourage mutually shared understanding require the healthcare interpreter to engage in explanation, cultural brokerage, and mediation when these actions are necessary" (p. 75). Kaufert and Putsch have expanded the views on interpreting skills to incorporate cultural brokering, negotiating, and teamwork (both with the patient and the patient's family and with the institution).

Examining English-ASL medical interviews, Metzger (1999) analyzes two cases and compares the influence that interpreters have on interpreted interactions. The first case is a pre-recorded role-play of a medical interview interpreted by an interpreting student. The second is an authentic interpreted medical interview facilitated by a professional interpreter. Metzger applies frame theory and Goffman's concept of footing (1981) to study whether an interpreter can interpret interactive discourse without influencing it. She concludes that interpreters have the power to influence interpreted discourse by misrepresenting the source-message footings with their renditions and also by interpreter-generated utterances.

Wadensjö (1998) also problematizes neutrality by addressing the distribution of responsibility among interlocutors. She looks mainly at how responsibility "for the progression and the substance of interaction is distributed in and through talk" (1998: 112). From her analysis of interpreted discourse, she concludes that the interpreter's role during the interaction goes beyond a traditional channel that simply conveys information. She says that interpreters co-construct meaning together with the interlocutors and that responsibility during interpretation is shared by all parties to the conversation. In this sense, the co-construction of meaning and the responsibility as team players within a conversation of both the interlocutors and the interpreter sheds light on other skills that interpreters display, beyond those of linguistic code switching and information processing. As is the case with Kaufert and Putsch, Wadensjö brings into the foreground the social skills utilized in interpreting that have been traditionally overlooked by the literature.

The quote by Marx at the beginning of this chapter reminds us that outward appearances of things do not necessarily portray their essence. So far in this discussion, we have considered interpreters as invisible language switchers, as co-participants, and as interlocutors whose visible role falls within a continuum of visibility. The linguistic gap in the ICE is not the only factor that determines the role of interpreters. The nature of any medical encounter, bilingual or mono-lingual, is in itself complex. In the next chapter, we will see how that complexity is influenced by the interpreter's visible role.

In the beginning is the relation.

Martin Buber, "I and Thou" (1970: 69)

The essence of the doctor–patient relationship

The term relationship refers to the condition of having a logical or natural association between two entities (*Random House Webster's Dictionary* 1997). From the cradle to the grave, human relationships are vital (Adler 2002). Every human relationship involves a connectedness between individuals, which is molded by both verbal and non-verbal communicative processes. Without communication, successful relationships would not be possible. In fact, even poor relationships depend greatly on communicative processes between individuals.

The importance of effective communication in the building of a successful relationship is well illustrated in the healthcare provider (HCP)–patient situation. Communication between HCP and patient encompasses both verbal and non-verbal interactions (Lee, Back, Block, and Stewart 2002). Although physicians of today are better educated and more scientific than ever before, they sometimes do not communicate effectively with their patients (Jacobs et al. 2001). This is particularly true in cases where HCPs and patients do not share the same cultural background. The diagnostic importance and therapeutic benefit of conversation between physician and patient has long been recognized. Research on the HCP–patient relationship tells us that better communication can improve patient satisfaction and clinical outcomes (Rosenberg, Lussier, and Beaudoin 1997).

When referring to the HCP–patient situation, it is important not to confuse the terms interaction and relationship. These two terms are not interchangeable. An interaction between patient and HCP is characterized by an observable exchange of behaviors, whereas a relationship involves qualities that are more subjective (caring, concern, respect, and compassion) (Zoppi and Epstein 2002). In *Medicine and the Family*, Candib (1995) discusses the ways in which clinicians can model caring relationships. She states that clinicians show caring through devotion and self-conduct, and it is their capacity for self-disclosure that reveals them as genuine. Frey (1998) asserts that, in terms of outcomes, the physician's relationship with the patient is more important than the actual delivery of medical care. Patients who are comfortable in their relationship with their physicians report greater satisfaction, decreased concern or worry about illness, adherence to treatment, and fewer requests for referrals to other physicians (Ferguson and Candib 2002; Zoppi and Epstein 2002). The distinction between interaction and relationship is of special importance when an interpreter becomes a part of the medical encounter. Is the interpreter part of an interaction (a specific encounter) or a relationship (an association defined by subjective qualities)? If the interpreter's participation is to be considered an integral part of a relationship, then who exactly are the partners?

According to Adler (2002), a collaborative relationship between physician and patient is a therapeutic alliance in which doctor and patient are partners engaged in a common struggle against an illness. Since this is not a part of the interpreter's job description, we must wonder: can a temporary guest (Angelelli 2000) to this struggle (i.e. an interpreter that switches from one ICE to another) be considered an essential part of the battle against illness? The HCP–patient collaboration increases the patient's autonomy, and this new, autonomous patient can make informed decisions. The establishment of an empathic bond, such as that described by Candib (1995), facilitates this collaboration, thus reducing the likelihood of a discordant relationship. A patient is less likely to lay blame on an empathic partner than on an impersonal paternalistic figure. The empathic bond also facilitates a positive sociophysiological co-processing of experience. This sociophysiological phenomenon, experienced as caring, makes the patient feel more comfortable. When patients are treated as partners in the medical dialogue, rather than as mere reporters of symptoms, they become more willing to ask questions or express concerns, and they are more likely to receive useful information about their illness and therapeutic plan. Adler (2002) says that a caring relationship between physician and patient can have many desirable results: a more complete medical history; improved clinical judgment and more accurate diagnoses; more cost-effective prescribing; a placebo response to pharmacotherapy; and a more satisfied and informed patient who is more likely to adhere to the treatment plan. The higher the quality of the HCP–patient relationship, the better the therapeutic outcomes.

But can a collaborative relationship between HCP and patient truly exist, especially across cultures? How does the presence of an interpreter affect this relationship? Does he/she improve it, or interfere, or, in fact, have no influence over it at all? The biopsychosocial paradigm of the doctor–patient relationship, first described by Engel (1988), focuses on patient-centered medicine and provides a guideline for sensitive healthcare. In this paradigm, exchanges between doctors and patients are referred to as patient-centered encounters, during which physicians not only try to understand the symptoms but also seek to facilitate patients' expressions of their thoughts, feelings, and expectations. Dialogue in the medical encounter is of utmost importance to the doctor–patient relationship, because it is "the only means whereby the patient can acquaint the physician with those inner experiences which had led him to consider himself ill in the first place" (p. 121). The patient-centered approach has been linked to improved patient and physician outcomes (Rivadeneyra, Elderkin-Thompson, Silver, and Waitzkin 2000).

Engel (1988) describes the function of the biopsychosocial model, and the key role of relationship and dialogue to its performance:

To appreciate relationship and dialogue as requirements for scientific study in the clinical setting highlights the natural confluence of the human and the scientific in the clinical encounter itself. It is not just that science is a human activity, it is also that the interpersonal engagement required in the clinical realm rests on complementary and basic human needs, especially the need to know and understand and the need to feel known and understood . . . For the patient, to feel understood by the physician means more than just feeling that the physician understands intellectually, that is, "comprehends," what the patient is reporting and what may be wrong, . . . Every bit as important is it that the physician display understanding about the patient as a person, as a fellow human being, and about what he is experiencing and what the circumstances of his life are. (pp. 124–5)

Roter (2002) explains that in the patient-centered encounter, the therapeutic dialogue is based on a biopsychosocial rather than a biomedical paradigm. In this setting, the patient is actively engaged in the medical dialogue, with the physician being open and responsive to the patient's viewpoint. The physician elicits the patient's concerns, expectations, and preferences for treatment, and emotional rapport is thus established. This approach, referred to as relationship-centered medicine (in order to more accurately reflect integration of the patient and physician perspective within the medical encounter), assists the physician in forming an empathic connection with patients regardless of ethnicity, gender, cultural background and identity, or life experience. When an interpreter enters the picture, both physician and patient sometimes find themselves addressing the interpreter instead of each other. What effect if any, then, might the interpreter's presence have on the dynamics of relationship-centered medicine?

Roter says that relationship-centered visits can be characterized as "medically functional, informative, facilitative, responsive, and participatory" (2002: 390). The term medically functional refers to the relationship's capacity to fulfill the medical management functions of the visit within the constraints of a given health delivery system.

The term "facilitative" refers to the ability of the relationship to elicit the patient's full spectrum of concerns and reason for the visit. The patient's telling of the story of his/her illness is the method by which the meaning of the illness and disease are integrated and interpreted by both doctor and patient. If the medical interpreter's rendition is expanded or summarized, we must ask ourselves whether this method is still viable. A patient's experience of illness is often reflected in how it affects family, social and professional functioning and relations, feelings, and emotions. The psychosocial realm of the experience can determine the patient's perspective in all subsequent care (Roter 2002).

Therefore, the medical encounter must be responsive to the patient's emotional state and concerns. Support, empathy, concern, and legitimation on the part of the physician, as well as focused questions regarding feelings and emotions, are important elements of rapport building. It is important for patients to feel that they are being heard and understood. Do interpreters who filter information that they feel is irrelevant stand in the way of this?

Most patients want as much information as possible from their physicians. They often seek both technical information and behavioral recommendations. Physicians must provide this information in a manner that is useful to the patient and easy to understand. When doctors do not speak the same language as their patients, they are forced to share this responsibility with interpreters. It is important that the patient be able to access this information, because: (1) it boosts the patient's capacity to cope with the uncertainty that goes along with having an illness, and (2) it helps to direct patient actions (Roter 2002).

The doctor–patient relationship should also be participatory. Physicians have an obligation to help patients assume a responsible role in decision making about their illnesses and therapies. However, not all patients, regardless of their culture of origin or language, are willing to take on such a responsibility. As we will see, the presence of an interpreter in the medical encounter adds to the complexity of this interaction, as the borders between who is actually taking the participatory roles (HCP, patient, or interpreter) become less clear.

Communication issues in a bilingual medical encounter

As Kaufert and Putsch (1997) have stated, medical discourse is not supposed to be adversarial. Its basic goal is mutual understanding. Clear verbal communication is a necessary component of an effective clinical encounter. Even when patients and providers are educated in the same language, faulty communication can lead to distortions and miscommunications between the two parties (Kaufert and Putsch 1997). Roter (2002) tells us that physician–patient communication becomes even more complicated "when the basic rules that govern communication are uncertain or unclear. This is the case when patients do not speak the same primary language as their physician, or when patients' limited literacy restricts their ability to understand and be understood by their physician" (p. 390).

According to the 2000 US Census, approximately 21 million people have limited proficiency in English (US Census 2000). There exists a vast ethnic and linguistic diversity in the US, which presents challenges for providing adequate healthcare for patients who have limited English-speaking ability. These patients cannot benefit from the fundamental interaction between HCP and patients because of language barriers (Jacobs et al. 2001). Language problems can hinder multiple aspects of healthcare, including access, health status, use of health services, and health outcomes. However, linguistic incompatibilities are not the only factors influencing healthcare. A patient's health beliefs and practices arise from a combination of normative cultural values together with personal experience and perceptions (Flores 2000; Hornberger et al. 1996). In other words, even when HCP and patient share the same language, the differences in their cultural norms can lead to miscommunications and misunderstandings.

Flores (2000) says that culture can have important clinical consequences in the patient–physician relationship. He notes that cultural differences, even without language differences, may impede effective communication and lead to misunderstandings. The same information can be construed differently, depending on how it is presented (Lee et al. 2002). While language differences can define group boundaries and distinguish its members from the rest of the world, culture consists of a framework of beliefs, symbols, and values often expressed through distinct language or the unique use of common language. Additionally, language-linked cultural norms may apply to broad categories of patients, including those identified by their ethnicity, gender, age cohort, sexual orientation, or religious beliefs (Roter 2002). Physicians often find themselves in situations in which their cultural beliefs and values differ from their patients', which hinders the establishment of the cooperative partnership (Lee et al. 2002).

Ferguson and Candib (2002) state that "further evidence supports the admonition that majority physicians need to be more effective in developing relationships and in their communication with ethnic and racial minority patients" (p. 353). It is important that a physician recognize and respond appropriately to a patient's normative cultural values. Failure to do so can result in a variety of adverse clinical consequences, for example access, health status, use of health services, and health outcomes (Flores 2000). Roter (2002) reminds us that "complex challenges are presented to physicians when assumptions regarding the social rules that govern communication are uncertain or unclear, as in the case of cross-cultural communication" (p. 390). The most important communication skills for an HCP in the cross-cultural setting are those that assist in patient assessment and elicitation skills to understand the patient's perspective of symptoms and explanatory health-belief models. When the doctor possesses these skills, the result is usually increased patient satisfaction, trust, and compliance (Ferguson and Candib 2002). For example, patients of different ethnic backgrounds vary in their preferences about how to hear news, especially bad news. Some cultures believe that even articulating bad news may be associated with adverse consequences. Most patients prefer to receive all available information about their disease and treatment options (Lee et al. 2002). It may be particularly important for physicians to openly address cross-cultural differences in patients' preferences about the delivery of bad news. Even patients who are interested in specific information, such as prognosis, may not ask questions. The authors remind us that physicians should not assume that patients automatically verbalize their questions when asked if they have any questions, nor that failure to verbalize reflects lack of interest in answers.

Ideally, all patients would be cared for by physicians who speak their language and share their culture (Flores 2000; Rivadeneyra et al. 2000). Research suggests that communicating with patients in their own language improves patient compliance and understanding of their disease (Manson 1988). According to Ferguson and Candib (2002), "the literature calls for a more diverse physician workforce since minority patients are more likely to choose minority physicians, to be more satisfied by language-concordant relationships, and to feel more connected and involved in decision making with racially-concordant physicians" (p. 353). Because this is not always possible, communication problems between doctors and patients who speak different languages are seen nationwide (Marcus 2003). Since, as some authors (Kuo and Fagan 1999; Rivadeneyra et al. 2000) point out, the quality of the physician–patient relationship affects the diagnosis, treatment, and recovery of patients, improved communication may improve the clinical outcome of patients who do not speak English.

The HCP–patient relationship is dependent on effective communication. In order to improve access to healthcare for limited-English-speaking patients, these patients need to be able to communicate adequately with their HCPs (Jacobs et al. 2001). Should the communication process be put at risk by physician–patient discordant-language encounters, the health status of non-English-speaking patients could be compromised. Cross-language encounters are slower and less precise than same-language medical encounters. Rivadeneyra et al. (2000) report that physicians cite lack of time as a hindrance in using the relationship-centered approach with their patients, even though they are aware of the fact that this approach has been linked to better medical outcomes.

Differences in race, ethnicity, and language all appear to affect the HCP–patient relationship. Ferguson and Candib (2002) assert that disparities in health outcomes among ethnic minority and racial groups have become increasingly clear. These authors believe that while the reasons for these disparities remain poorly understood, the doctor–patient relationship may be an important factor. According to Flores (2000), "failure to consider a patient's cultural and linguistic issues can result in inaccurate histories, decreased satisfaction with care, non-adherence, poor continuity of care, less preventive screening, miscommunication, difficulties with informed consent, inadequate analgesia, a lower likelihood of having a primary care provider, decreased access to care, use of harmful remedies, delayed immunizations, and fewer prescriptions" (p. 21).

Some authors (Ferguson and Candib 2002; Flores 2000) have reported that clinicians sometimes provide a lower quality of care to patients from different cultures. Minority patients, especially those not proficient in English, are less likely to engender empathic response from physicians, establish rapport with physicians, receive sufficient information, and be encouraged to participate in medical decision making. Jacobs et al. (2001) report that patients who cannot speak English well receive less than optimal healthcare and are at greater risk of not receiving preventive care and other services. Patients in cross-linguistic encounters are likely to find their providers less friendly and less respectful than do patients without a language barrier, which is likely to reduce the desire of these patients to seek out the same HCP to establish trusting, professional relationships (Rivadeneyra et al. 2000).

Navigating across languages and cultures: the need for interpreters

According to Hornberger et al. (1996), patients' inability to speak the same language as their physicians or other HCPs compromises their access to care and the quality of that care. Non-English-speaking patients in the US have fewer primary care visits and receive fewer preventive services, although it is uncertain which factors (patient or provider) explain their lower use of preventive services and poorer health status. Patients in cross-linguistic encounters are more likely to make emergency room visits. Rivadeneyra et al. (2000) believe that this could be because non-English-speaking patients may prefer waiting until a problem becomes severe rather than trying to explain symptoms to someone who speaks a different language. These same authors assert that the communication barrier between non-English-speaking patients and their HCPs extends beyond just language difficulties. Both physicians and patients may change their behavior in subtle ways that may compromise the development of a trusting relationship. This situation both increases the likelihood of physicians misunderstanding patients' descriptions of their symptoms, and decreases the probability that patients will adhere to physicians' recommendations.

According to Ferguson and Candib (2002), "minority patients, especially those not proficient in English, are less likely to engender empathic responses from physicians, less likely to establish rapport with physicians, less likely to receive sufficient information, and less likely to be encouraged to participate in medical decision making" (p. 353).

Taking into consideration the complexity of the medical encounter, can the relationship ever develop between an HCP and a patient who do not share language or culture? As we have already seen, a relationship is quite different from an interaction or an encounter. What means, if any, can be used to bridge this gap that exists in communication between HCPs and patients? The majority of the information physicians use to determine a diagnosis and develop a therapeutic plan is gathered during the medical history which is, of course, more challenging when the physician and patient do not have a common language. Communicating with patients in their own language improves patient compliance and understanding of their disease. Since good communication helps doctors, patients, and their family members to work together successfully, various strategies for improving access for limited-English-speaking patients have been formulated. These include: (1) care by physicians or medical residents who are bilingual; (2) use of bilingual support staff; (3) use of bilingual employees who interpret in addition to their regular work; (4) use of professional interpreters; and (5) use of the speakerphone to provide language interpreting (Barnett 2002; Ferguson and Candib 2002; García 2000; and Kuo and Fagan 1999).

Most institutions rely extensively on untrained interpreters. Ginsberg et al. (1995) reported on a survey carried out in eighty-three public and private hospitals by the National Public Health and Hospital Institute. Less than a quarter of hospitals were shown to offer any interpreting training for their staff. Only nine hospitals trained their volunteer interpreters. This tells us that most hospital interpreting is performed by patients, family, friends, and hospital staff, all of whom are untrained in interpreting. This practice, also referred to as *ad hoc* interpreting, often results in errors in interpreting (omissions, additions, and substitutions) and condensations of what was said by both the clinician and the patient (Flores 2000; Baker et al. 1998; Jacobs et al. 2001).

Ad hoc interpreters have also been said to make behavioral mistakes that may affect both patient and physician satisfaction. It is not unusual for family members to accompany patients, especially elderly patients, to their medical visits. These visits, however, differ from those involving just the doctor and patient. The mere presence of someone other than the physician and patient in the medical consult introduces a whole new set of psychosocial factors into the equation, posing a risk for the physician–patient relationship. Campbell et al. (2002) argue that patients who are accompanied by a family member are likely to behave differently than unaccompanied patients in relation to their medical problems, functional abilities, family relationships, and attitudes toward family involvement in their care. In a study by Baker et al. (1998), family members acting as interpreters responded frequently to questions without allowing the patient to answer, volunteered their own information and opinions, and failed to interpret certain comments made by the patient. Physicians' questions were often misinterpreted or not interpreted at all, which in some cases resulted in misdiagnosis. Inadequate interpreting also impaired patient–provider communication about diagnosis and treatment. Any or all of these behaviors, plus the fact that both HCPs and patients often look at the person doing the interpreting during the clinical encounter instead of looking at one another, may put distance between patient and HCP. Lack of eye contact between physicians and patients may lessen providers' awareness of non-verbal clues about patients' thoughts and feelings, thus compromising the taking of the clinical history. *Ad hoc* services have many negative clinical consequences including "reduced trust in physicians, lower patient satisfaction, and breach of patient confidentiality, inaccurate communication, misdiagnosis, inadequate or inaccurate treatment, and reduced quality of care" (Jacobs et al. 2001: 469). On the other hand, a study by Kuo and Fagan (1999) showed that patients had high levels of satisfaction and comfort when they use family members and friends as interpreters, and that patients from certain cultures may even prefer their use to unfamiliar interpreters. These authors point out some advantages of *ad hoc* interpreters, for instance, they are a readily available, inexpensive source of information, and they can also assist the patient with tasks such as arranging transportation and follow-up visits.

Family members accompanying patients play roles that go beyond providing language assistance. They offer comfort and, when it comes to interpreting, they automatically count on having the patient's trust. The job of the interpreter goes beyond building trust. Interpreters set up and explain their own role at the outset of a medical encounter. Ideally, they transmit information accurately and completely and manage the flow of communication between all participants. Interpreters also manage the dynamics of the medical encounter by encouraging patient and doctor to address each other directly. Finally, they assist with closure activities such as follow-up instructions and patient referral to auxiliary services (Baker et al. 1998).

Even when interpreters are available, there is often little or no standardization in interpreter training, assessment of competence, or instruction of healthcare providers in how to use an interpreter (Baker et al. 1998). These authors concede that several states have passed laws or established regulations requiring HCPs to have interpreters or bilingual staff available for patients who need them (Massachusetts Medical Interpreters Association [MMIA] 1996; California Healthcare Interpreter Association [CHIA] 2002). "These laws and regulations, however, do not define what constitutes adequate screening, testing, training, and proficiency for interpreters," assert Baker et al. (1998: 1469). Select policy-making bodies have attempted to define the standards of practice and role of the interpreter in the medical setting. The MMIA, for example, has established standards of practice for medical interpreters to help decrease interpreting errors and to diminish behaviors that adversely affect the patient–provider relationship (MMIA 1996). Another example of standardization can be found in California, where in 2001 the California Standards for Healthcare Interpreters were established in response to the passing of legislative requirements calling for the use of interpreters in that state (CHIA 2002).

According to Jacobs et al. (2001), interpreting services have the potential to increase provision of clinical, therapeutic, and preventive services through three mechanisms: (1) enhanced patient and physician understanding; (2) enhanced physician–patient trust; and (3) patient satisfaction. Enhanced patient and physician understanding motivates patients to make and keep appointments. It also gives physicians more confidence in their diagnoses and in the patient's understanding of the risks and benefits of a particular treatment. Patients are more likely to get their prescriptions filled, because they understand both the purpose of the treatment and the instructions for taking the medication. Enhanced physician–patient trust is established by effective communication. This two-way trust is dependent upon understanding, caring, clear communication, partnership building, and question answering.

While most studies support the idea that professional interpreters are more likely to bridge the gaps in healthcare access experienced by non-English-speaking patients, Ferguson and Candib (2002) demonstrated persistently poor communication skills on the part of the physicians, in spite of the presence of interpreters. Poorly organized medical-language services can discourage non-English-speaking persons from seeking appropriate healthcare. Although interpreters are important for both the physician and the patient, the patient assumes the bulk of the negative consequences (avoidable morbidity or mortality) related to poor outcomes resulting from ineffective communication when interpreter services are not used or are used improperly.

When an interpreter is assigned to serve as intermediary in a medical encounter, both practical and ethical problems can arise (Kaufert and Putsch 1997). The presence or absence of an interpreter affects the encounter in various ways. The presence of an interpreter reduces the direct verbal communication and non-verbal reciprocity between doctor and patient, thus rendering the encounter less personal, decreasing patients' sense of connection to their provider. This is especially the case when HCPs have not been taught how to use an interpreter (Baker et al. 1998; Rivadeneyra et al. 2000). According to Baker et al. (1998), the presence of a third party may negatively affect the relationship (because of a decreased sense of privacy and intimacy between patient and physician), even when the interpreter and the clinician have optimal training in how to function in this situation. The authors found that patients who communicated through an interpreter were less likely to know their diagnosis and more likely to say they wished the provider had explained better, whereas patients who were able to communicate directly with their provider demonstrated more satisfaction. Patients who communicated through an interpreter also rated their provider as less friendly, less respectful, less concerned for the patient as a person, and less likely to take measures to make the patient feel comfortable.

Despite the fact that difficulties arise when communicating through an interpreter, even greater negative consequences can be seen when an interpreter is not used. Jacobs et al. (2001) have shown that professional interpreter services increase delivery of healthcare to limited-English-speaking patients in a model health-maintenance organization with a large staff. In this study, patients who used the interpreter services had a significantly greater increase in office visits, prescription writing, and prescription filling compared to a control group.

Jacobs et al. remind us that it is important to be mindful of the fact that the findings of only a few studies may not be generalizable to all clinics or all languages. Cultural differences as well as language proficiency may independently influence patients' expectations for satisfactory medical care. However, the findings of these studies cannot be ignored. The fact remains that cultural, educational, and economic barriers exist for many limited-English-speaking patients. As the authors state, "providing these patients with the means to inform [their healthcare providers] about their symptoms and concerns and to navigate healthcare delivery systems is an important step toward improving their health" (2001: 473).

At the beginning of this chapter, the essence of a relationship was described by the association between two entities. In the medical encounter, then, how does the presence of a family member or interpreter affect the establishment of the doctor–patient relationship? How can a relationship be established between doctor and patient when there is a third party involved? And who is the relationship between? Doctor and patient? Doctor and interpreter? Patient and interpreter? Is there such a thing as a three-party interaction, a communicative *pas-de-trois* (Wadensjö 1998) for a relationship-centered medical visit? And even if there is, can the formation of alliances between any two members of the three-way interaction be avoided? Moreover, does it need to be avoided? If an HCP requests the same interpreter for each cross-linguistic medical interaction, then isn't the HCP establishing the relationship with the interpreter? How, then, can the interpreter remain neutral in the encounter, and not form an alliance with the HCP? Can alliances be formed between patient and interpreter? As we have seen, communicating through an interpreter can be a double-edged sword. When used improperly, it can pose a barrier to establishing a therapeutic patient–provider relationship. However, adequate communication brokered through an interpreter can facilitate the exchange of information between HCP and patient and have a profoundly positive impact on the wellbeing of the patient. In the next chapter, we will review various theories on communicative events, at whose intersection lies the ICE, as we look at the role of the interpreter through different lenses.

3   A different set of lenses

A curious analogy could be based on the fact that even the hugest telescope
has to have an eye-piece no larger than the eye.

Ludwig Wittgenstein, *Culture and Value* (1980: 17e)

Looking at the interpreter's role through different lenses

In chapters 1 and 2, we have examined a paradigm shift: from the interpreter as
a conduit of information to a co-participant in the interaction. This shift helps
to describe how interpreters do their jobs, but it does not tell us why interpreters
make the choices they make. If they are co-participants, then what triggers their
participation? Interpreters are full participants in communicative interactions
together with doctors and patients. Like any of the other co-participants, interpreters bring their social baggage (their beliefs, attitudes, and cultural norms) to
the medical encounter, and they exercise their agency. Interpreters, like all other
human beings, participate in an interaction that does not happen in a social vacuum. Regardless of whether they perform the prescribed role or whether they
become more visible by directing the flow of communication, their performance is constrained by the institution and the society in which the interaction
is embedded. This inescapable fact has not yet been fully addressed (the exception being Davidson 2001). The interpreter's agency is present at three levels:
interpersonal, institutional, and societal.

In the case of a doctor–patient interview in a public hospital, the doctor most
likely belongs to the more dominant culture while the patient may belong to the
less dominant culture. The interpreter in this situation may have more social
factors in common with one party or with the other, but clearly not with both.
Under such circumstances, how can we expect these individuals to remain truly
neutral? We can turn to three bodies of knowledge to help us better understand
the interpreter's role in an ICE: (1) social theory; (2) sociological theory; and
(3) linguistic anthropology. Figure 4 shows the interplay of lenses we can use
to approach the different levels of the ICE.

For the institutional and societal level, I draw from Bourdieu's theory of
practice (1977, 1990, 1991). Theories in interpersonal relations include: (1) the

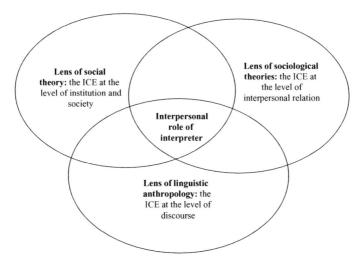

Figure 4   Multiple lenses to look at the interpreter in an ICE

theory on impression formation (Brewer 1988; Feagin 1991; Rosenhan 1973);
(2) social comparison theory (Festinger 1954); (3) the theory of the significant
other; (4) attribution theory (Fiske and Taylor 1991); (5) affect-control theory
(Candace 1990; Hochschild 1983; Ridgeway 1993; Sacther and Singer 1962;
Smith-Lovin 1990); and status characterization theory (Webster and Foschi
1998). The literature from linguistic anthropology includes: Niebhur 1963;
Duranti 1992; Hill and Irvine 1992; Hill and Zepeda 1992; Hymes 1974; and
Irvine 1992.

The lens of society and the institution

According to Bourdieu's theory of practice, each ICE is shaped not only by its
participants but also by the past, present, and future dispositions that each participant brings to the encounter (e.g. doctors examining patients; patients seeking assistance; interpreters offering linguistic or cultural competence). This
theory explains how an interaction cannot be considered independent from the
objective structures to which it owes its form. These structures have produced
the dispositions (*habitus*) (1977: 81) of the interacting agents and have allotted
them their relative positions in the interaction. In essence, habitus produces conscious practices. These practices are secured by a consensus, a common sense
of perceiving them on the part of the agents. This consensus produces the homo-
geneity of the habitus. The habitus becomes an immanent law. For Bourdieu,
relationships are never just about the individuals involved. Instead, each relationship must be viewed in terms of all of the social factors that each individual

brings with her/him and all of the constraints that are placed upon these individuals by the institutions and societies in which the relationship takes place.

The theory of practice thus sheds a different light on the role of the interpreter. Interpreters, like any other human beings, also have a habitus and are constrained by the institutions within which they interact. But, are the forces that impinge on the interpersonal role of the interpreter generated only at the institutional level? Or is the institution embedded in a bigger set of forces?

Beyond the institution one may work for, as members of a given society, we tend to conform to beliefs, norms, and rules of the society where we live. Interpreters, as members of a society, are no exception to this. This may mean that we grow up inheriting certain social values from our own families and communities, and then we construct, co-construct, and reconstruct them as we navigate through life. Some social values get to be re-enacted as others are challenged or dropped. By judging certain behaviors as acceptable or unacceptable or by deciding whether we conform more to one point of view or another, we may align more and less with certain social groups. We make choices and we build allegiances by exercising our agency. So does the interpreter. These choices may appear to be conscious or unconscious at different times, but regardless of our awareness, we enact them as we contribute to building our share of the societal fabric. Pretending that any of us could escape this is as fictitious as pretending that any of us could be placed in a social vacuum.

As discussed previously, Bourdieu's theory of practice also explains how "interpersonal relations are never, except in appearance, individual-to-individual relationships and that the truth of the interaction is never entirely contained in the interaction" (1977: 81). At a societal level, Bourdieu (1991) uses economic terms to analyze forms of interaction that are not strictly economic transactions. In the field of cross-cultural and linguistic communication the orientation is more towards other kinds of capital such as cultural or symbolic power.

Any communication (mono- or multilingual) is a linguistic exchange, which in itself is an economic exchange (Bourdieu 1991). This economic exchange materializes within a symbolic relation of power. The doctor is a producer, endowed with knowledge that the patient needs. The patient is somewhat less powerful. Where, then, does that leave the interpreter? The interpreter, endowed with bilingual ability, is also a producer, and the monolingual interlocutors are the consumers. This means that bilingual persons, who have had diverse cultural experiences, may be endowed with a linguistic habitus that allows them to interact with ease with different linguistic, and even sometimes, class backgrounds. They can communicate with, for example, a doctor and a patient, tailoring not only the language but also the register to make it appropriate to both interlocutors during the same exchange.

The lens of social theory helps us understand the ICE in the bigger context, allowing us to place the participants within an institution and a society. It helps us conceive the interpreter and the manifestations of the interpersonal role in a broader sense, with his/her tendencies and limitations. The interpreter, like any other agent and member of a society who works within an institution, is not an exception to this and cannot therefore escape from this interconnection. This helps us understand that the interpreter has both a habitus and agency in the behaviors. However, the social theory lens does not focus on the interaction of the interpreter, who, as social being, interacts with others. In order to do this, we must turn to the lens of sociological theories.

The lens of the interaction

When two or more interlocutors interact, they bring to the interaction the self. The aforementioned theories on social psychology state that people depend on one another in two ways: (1) effect dependent (they come together to achieve goals); and (2) information dependent (they depend on each other to gather information about their environment). In the case of medical interpreting, the three parties (HCP, patient, and interpreter) come together for both reasons: they need to achieve communication, and they need to gather information about a situation.

For example, they come together because they need to achieve the wellbeing of the patient. In order to achieve this goal, they depend on each other to gather information. Each participant contributes something unique to the ICE: for the HCP, it is scientific knowledge; for the interpreter, it is interpreting skill; for the patient, it is the description of his/her illness. At first contact, each individual forms an impression of each one of the others, based on social factors (gender, race, and age) that are evident, even before a single word is uttered. The theory of impression formation (Brewer 1988) states that when people come together, they need to define *self* and *other* so that they can interact. However, the colossal amount of information in the world forces us to attend selectively to information according to a system of categories, which causes us to never perceive anything directly or fully. Our sense of the world is mediated by our system of categories, meaning that everyone sees the world through various lenses and creates the picture and meanings of what they see. Everything seen is as much the product of the world as it is of any individual's or group's system of categories. The category system applied by any single individual to the world, in order to make sense of it, is a result of cultural and class backgrounds as well as ethnicity and gender. Cultural schema in particular include institutionalized settings (the cultural rules and roles that people are supposed to play) and social accounts (what each society believes).

In applying any system of categories, human beings engage in impression formation (Brewer 1988). In doing so, they must balance simplicity, accuracy, and self-esteem. Simplicity is important, because human beings like to categorize immediately. It is necessary to store the information in an orderly way. The information must be accurate, even if it is simple. If the wrong category is applied to a person, that person may resist the category, creating a problem. I say *may* resist, because not everybody can engage in category resistance. Since category resistance is linked to power, a person who has more power or status in a relationship will be more capable of resisting categories (Feagin 1991; Rosenhan 1973). While managing the tension between simplicity and accuracy, people who are interacting still care about maintaining self-esteem; the self is the most important element in the interaction.

According to Brewer (1988), the process of impression formation has the following stages: (1) identification; (2) typing and sub-typing; (3) individuation; and (4) personalization. Except for personalization, all stages are top-down. The point at which the process is stopped correlates with the amount of involvement expected of each of the parties in the interaction. Therefore, the degree of involvement in a situation determines the efforts that will go into personalization or individuation. The first set of categories marks the nature of the interaction.

Once the parties involved in the medical encounter have categorized one another (i.e. the impression has been formed), they proceed to categorize each other based on each individual's cultural schema. In social comparison theory, Festinger (1954) says that people rely on one another to try to make sense of reality. We compare impressions of what is real, in order to construct a social definition of reality. The confidence and sense of security of the self is based on others' acknowledgment that the self is on target as to the perception of reality. Festinger (1954) claims that we are inclined to compare information with socially oriented peers (people with whom we share the same social location). We also take the information received from these peers as accurate. This is particularly important for social influence. Following Festinger's claims, we can see that the other is to the social self what the mirror is to the physical self. In other words, the other is the mirror of the social self.

This construct of social influence was also explored by the theory of the significant other (Stouffer et al. 1949), which discussed how self is rooted and anchored in social relations. People become so influential to one another that they go to extremes when the self becomes vulnerable. The self may change according to what significant others think is right or wrong. Examples of the effect of this extreme influence are cults, brainwashing, and extreme isolation where people change their patterns of relations, ultimately resulting in a change of the self. But even though the self is vulnerable to those influences, the self is an active agent too. The self has control over those with whom it decides to interact. This control is affected by the position of the self, *vis à vis* the other, in terms of power and status. Basically, the self is restrained by the social position. The more power the self has, the more it can avoid being compared negatively to others. Inequalities are perpetuated in this way, since the poor and the powerless are constantly labeled. When the self and the other start interacting, sometimes the lens of attribution theory is used to understand the reality of the interaction (Fiske and Taylor 1991). It shows that when the effect of an action is distinctive or unusual, people engage in correspondent inference. We attribute causes to the reality of the interaction. This can happen, for example, in a socially undesirable situation.

Of course, the formation of these impressions and the subsequent inter-action (i.e. individuals engaging in the attribution process) are not free of biases or errors. Fiske and Taylor (1991) classified these biases and errors into six different types: (1) fundamental attribution error; (2) actor–observer bias; (3) self-serving bias; (4) false consensus effect; (5) defensive attributions; and (6) self-centered bias. The fundamental attribution error occurs when one is biased towards making internal, rather than external, attributions to a behavior. Labeling someone as rude, uncooperative, or careless is quicker and easier than analyzing the external factors that prompted a person to behave in a certain way.

The actor–observer bias refers to the attributions that an observer makes about an actor's behavior in a particular situation. The actor almost always has more information than the observer. The actor is more inclined to consider the circumstances in which the behavior occurred and make external attributions. The observer tends to be more biased, making internal attributions and plac-ing blame on others. Thus, there is always tension between the actor and the observer.

The self-serving bias is reflected by the fact that we tend to take credit for the successes and attribute failure to circumstances. Basically this bias is related to whatever flatters the self in a given situation. Thus, this bias is tied to self-esteem.

The false consensus effect is based on the assumption that social reality is shared. It is also related to social comparison theory. It becomes exagger-ated when we become threatened. This is because agreeing with people makes socially constructed reality more secure.

Defensive attributions are related to the just world hypothesis. Human beings tend to attribute responsibility to people for actions that produce severe con-sequences. Severe consequences dictate holding others more responsible. This allows us to make scary events predictable, thus making us feel safer, more secure. It is this defense mechanism that causes people to blame the victim of a situation, rather than to analyze the circumstances that led to it.

Self-centered bias consists of taking more than one's share of responsibility for a jointly achieved outcome. This differs from the self-serving bias in the sense that it does not distinguish between success and failure. The self always takes a bigger share, regardless of whether the outcome is positive or negative.

It is important to mention that as we interact, our actions and attributions have emotional consequences. Emotions, which are socially constructed by the cultural beliefs and schemas of our society, shape our reactions to our own actions and to those of others and have consequences and implications on the interaction (Ridgeway 1994).

Another consequence of the categorization of human beings by other human beings is that each individual receives a different status. In the HCP–patient–interpreter triad, the status of each person depends on the information he/she brings to the encounter. Apart from perceptions, attributions, feelings, and emotions, the factor that may be most influential in the interaction of the triad is status. The lens of status generalization theory states that relations are influenced by the social categories to which we belong, as well as by the cultural beliefs attached to those categories. Status is an exchange. The self gives deference to the other, because the other has something that is meaningful to the self. This triggers the formation of hierarchies within the group (Webster and Foschi 1998). The meaningful element that the other possesses (e.g. knowledge, information) must be meaningful to and valued by the group (patient, HCP, and interpreter). Otherwise, we are not in the presence of status, but rather dominance. The difference between status and dominance is that in the former, the person who enjoys higher status is collectively defined as the more capable of achieving a collective goal. The self gives deference to the other, thus enabling the other to achieve the collective goal for the group.

The theories we have reviewed do not conceive the individual as someone who is indifferent to another person's reaction or to the social milieu. On the contrary, they portray an individual who perceives and reacts to those perceptions with agency. In this sense, the individual is anything but neutral to instances of power, discrimination, conference, or deference of status. These theories portray a person who is engaged in social interaction, builds interpersonal relations, and behaves according to emotions, perceptions, and information sought and obtained. Because these theories have been applied to persons in general, it is appropriate to include the interpreter, who is a person and who is a participant in the medical encounter. The interpreter undergoes all the same processes as the other parties upon making initial contact. The interpreter is also subject to instances of power and dominance and high or low status, in the same way as the monolingual parties. The portraying of an interpreter as neutral and invisible can be considered fictitious in light of the lens of sociological theory.

The two sets of lenses we have used so far (social theory and sociological theory) have helped us understand how any interpreting event is socially bound and constrained, as are its participants. They have allowed us to see the interpreter within the interaction in which he/she participates, and the interaction within the bigger picture into which it is inserted (either the hospital or the society). We have yet to see how interpreters are also visible through their own words (see chapters 6 and 7). We will now use the lens of linguistic anthropology to help us look at manifestations of the interpersonal role of the interpreter at the micro-level.

The lens of discourse

The lens of linguistic anthropology allows us to approach the ICE at the level of discourse, enabling us to conceive an interlocutor embedded in a speech community (Hymes 1974). Hymes' taxonomy of speaking (1974) can be used to define a communicative event. He defines a communicative event (1974: 10) in terms of the factors that constitute it: (1) the participants (e.g. senders and receivers); (2) the channels and their modes of use (e.g. speaking, writing); (3) the various codes shared by the participants (e.g. linguistic, kinesic); (4) the settings in which communication is permitted or encouraged; (5) the forms of messages and their genres (from single-morpheme sentences to organized routines and styles); (6) the attitudes and contents of a message; and (7) the events themselves.

Hymes' theory of speaking considers as fundamental the notions of ways of speaking, speaker, speech community, speech situation, speech event, speech act, rules of speaking, and function of speech. He also analyzes the following speech components (1974: 53–62):

1. Message form. How something is said by members in a given speech community and according to the descriptive characteristics outlined above.
2. Message content. Topic and change of topic.
3. Setting. The time and place of a speech act and, in general, the physical circumstances.
4. Scene. The cultural definition of an occasion; the psychological setting.
5. Participants. May include the following: speaker or sender; addressor; hearer, receiver, or audience; addressee.
6. Purpose, outcomes. The expected outcome of a speech event as recognized by the speech community.
7. Purposes, goals. The intentions of participants, and the strategies they define.
8. Key. Tone, manner, or spirit of a speech act (e.g. seriousness, sarcasm).
9. Channels. The medium of speech transmission (e.g. oral, written, visual).
10. Forms of speech. The different languages, dialects, varieties, and registers used in a speech event or act; may be joined with channels as means or agencies of speaking.

11. Norms of interaction. Rules governing speaking.
12. Norms of interpretation. The belief system of a community and how that interacts with the frame of references for understanding utterances.
13. Genres. Categories of speech (e.g. poem, myth, tale, proverb, riddle, curse, prayer, oration, lecture). Though often coincidental with speech event, genres must be treated as analytically independent.

In a monolingual medical communicative event (e.g. an interview between a HCP and a patient), we can assume that the HCP is familiar with the ways of speaking that occur in his/her own speech community (the medical environment). Undoubtedly, this means that the HCP is a fluent speaker of that speech community. The same holds true for the patient, who belongs to a different speech community, in which the ways of speaking of its members are distinct from those of the HCP. Thus in any example of a communicative event between HCP and patient, the interlocutors do not usually share a speech community. To illustrate the application of these terms to describe an actual medical encounter, we can use the example of a communicative event in which the doctor and patient are discussing a patient's upcoming surgical procedure. In this example, the speech situation is the conversation between the HCP and the patient (both belonging to different speech communities) about the upcoming surgical procedure and related health issues. The speech event is an exchange during that interview (the doctor explains the procedure to the patient). The speech act is a remark during that interview (tone, irony, e.g. the patient's use of irony to express frustration at the unnecessary complexity of the pre-operative interview process).

Monolingual and interpreted communicative events: differences and similarities

Hymes' approach to communication is comprehensive and complex. But, how does it help us understand communication via interpreting? Table 1, based on Hymes' fundamental notions, illustrates the differences and similarities between a monolingual communicative event (MCE) and an ICE (Angelelli 2000).

As can be seen in the table, the differences between the MCE and the ICE are numerous. We will now discuss the most salient differences.

• *Scene*. During an ICE, the interpreter may explore the psychological settings that the two parties do not have in common. The interpreter's constant interaction with both speaker and listener allows for negotiation and clarification. The interpreter is a key player in this discovery. He/she may even become a gatekeeper *vis à vis* the parties, should he/she decide *not* to explore this, since the individual parties may not discover the scene on their own. On the

Table 1 *Fundamental notions of monolingual and interpreted communicative events*

Hymes' components of speech	Monolingual communicative event in a hospital setting	Interpreted communicative event in a hospital setting
Setting: the time and place of a speech act and, in general, the physical circumstances.	**Setting:** the physical circumstances of a speech event (such as time and place) are evident to the interlocutors. They do not mean the same to both. HCP is more familiar with the setting than P. P and HCP are at opposite extremes of a familiarity continuum. Time, place, and physical circumstances of the speech act play an essential role in communication as they provide the context for what is being said.	**Setting:** the physical circumstances of a speech event (such as time and place) are not equally evident to the three interlocutors. The setting plays an essential role in communication by providing the context for what is being said, even if it is not constructed in the same way. HI may be more familiar with the setting than P. If we place HI in a continuum of familiarity with the setting, and if HCP is at the familiar extreme and P at the unfamiliar one, HI is closer to HCP's end.
Scene: the cultural definition of an occasion; the psychological setting.	**Scene:** HCP and P may not share it completely, as they do not belong to the same speech community. One (HCP) is a more permanent dweller than the other. P only interacts in this scene every time he/she communicates with an HCP.	**Scene:** HCP, P, and HI may not share it completely, as they do not belong to the same speech community. It might be more accessible or evident for HI than for P (who might be used to a different scene in his own culture), as the former explores it not so much as an outsider does but as a discovering party. The situation allows for clarification.
Participants: may include the following: speaker, sender; addressor; hearer, receiver, or audience; addressee.	**Speaker or sender:** Both HCP and P may become speakers. The power differential between HCP and P, however, makes HCP perform the role of speaker more often.	**Speaker or sender:** HI becomes the speaker and the listener in embedded dialogues as P and HCP become listeners and speakers. HI becomes speaker even more often than HCP while brokering communication between the two monolingual parties, especially when engaged in explanation of technical terms or cultural adaptations. HI also becomes listener more times than the other two interlocutors.

(*cont.*)

Table 1 (*cont.*)

Hymes' components of speech	Monolingual communicative event in a hospital setting	Interpreted communicative event in a hospital setting
	Hearer, or receiver or audience: the interaction between HCP and P is constant. It is always possible to negotiate meaning directly but power differentials are in place.	**Hearer, or receiver or audience:** HI becomes the hearer or receiver of every utterance. There is almost no verbal interaction between P and HCP except through HI.
	Addressee: the addressor/speaker (HCP/P)identifies the addressees (HCP/P) in each exchange. HCP/P are able to see how the message and event may be anticipated at its destination. (Does P understand the importance of the question? Is HCP going to feel compassion at P's tone?)	**Addressee:** Because P and HCP do not share a language, HI identifies the addressee. In doing this, HI is able to see how the message and event may be anticipated at their destination. (Is P going to understand this term? Is HCP going to be puzzled by the use of this home remedy?) HI is playing multiple roles as speaker/hearer/addressee and interpreter in each exchange.
Purposes/outcomes: the expected outcome of a speech event as recognized by the speech community.	**Purposes/outcomes:** the parties negotiate the outcomes of the event directly (is P going to consent to the surgery or not?). There is possibility for direct negotiation and the parties are familiar with the outcomes (e.g. HCP talks to P directly about his/her healthcare issues and uses technical language). Turning the negotiation into a learning process/experience for P or HCP is not expected. Talking to family members first or bypassing the patient is not acceptable or expected.	**Purposes/outcomes:** HI cannot do the job if he/she does not understand what the particular outcome of the communicative event is. (Is it an interview to make a decision about the surgery or is it an interview to prepare for the surgery?) This three-party negotiation adds more layers to the complexity of expectancy present in a monolingual interview. Outcomes of the relationship between P and HCP vary across languages and cultures. HI needs to be attuned to them and negotiate them as they emerge (e.g. HIs may need to alert parties to issues that are not acceptable across cultures as they also engage in lengthy explanations about the issues discussed). This means there are more embedded purposes than those of the original speech event.

Table 1 (*cont.*)

Hymes' components of speech	Monolingual communicative event in a hospital setting	Interpreted communicative event in a hospital setting
Purposes/goals: the intentions of participants and the strategies they define.	**Purposes/goals:** the intentions of the participants and the strategies defined during the medical interview are expressed directly. (Who is making the decision on the surgery? Who will the decision affect and how is that party accommodating to the making of that decision?) Power differentials are played out by P and HCP.	**Purposes/goals:** HI focuses on each of the participant's intentions, on their goals within the outcome and intends to portray them across gulfs of languages and cultures (why is P not willing to have a direct discussion on a life/death decision? Why does HCP need to have it?). At the same time the presence of HI generates other goals that need to be considered during the speech event.
Message form: how something is said by members in a given speech community and according to the descriptive characteristics outlined above.	**Message form:** because participants do share a language but not necessarily a speech community, they can resort to language to broker and bridge the forms in which something is said. If, however, P is too shy to ask a question, he/she will leave the interview with doubt, since there is nobody else to act on his/her behalf. If HCP is too abrupt in breaking bad news, the abruptness will reach P intact.	**Message form:** "the more a way of speaking has become shared and meaningful within a group, the more likely that crucial clues will be efficient" (p. 55). It would be reasonable to say then that HI, by virtue of being a quasi-community member, could be familiar with how members of the HCP community speak. HI, then, could be aware of the competence that speakers of the HCP community have and share in order to be able to go beyond the content of an explicit statement. HI is, in general, also familiar with how P speaks even when there is variation among Ps. In this sense, HI has an advantage over both monolingual parties for being familiar with one or more of the forms in which messages are uttered. HI is also adding another layer of message forms when he/she explains, mitigates, brokers, the form of the message.
Message content: topic and change of topic.	**Message content:** the participants can follow a topic and a change of topic by carefully following the	**Message content:** apparently the message content is more concrete than the message form and therefore it might be more

(*cont.*)

Table 1 (*cont.*)

Hymes' components of speech	Monolingual communicative event in a hospital setting	Interpreted communicative event in a hospital setting
	meaning of what is being said. This does not mean that it is comprehensible to both but the monolingual situation allows for direct negotiation.	accessible to a quasi-member of a community. HI can follow a topic and a change of topic by carefully following the meaning of what is being said. The other participants cannot and depend on HI to do this. HI adds another layer of content as he/she explains, mitigates, brokers.
Key: tone, manner, or spirit of a speech act (e.g. seriousness, sarcasm).	**Key:** HCP and P, focus on the tone, manner, or spirit of the other interlocutor.	**Key:** HI focuses on the tone, manner, or spirit of the each of the other two interlocutors. HI's utterances add a third component of key to the ICE.
Channels: the medium of speech transmission (e.g. oral, written, telegraphic).	**Channels:** the participants have only one mode of input and that is each other's utterances.	**Channels:** HI has only one mode of input, the oral channel that at times can be split into two threads (one for each participant when they overlap). Plus, HI adds another thread as his/her utterances are expressed via the oral mode.
Forms of speech: the different languages, dialects, varieties, and registers used in a speech event/act; may be joined with channels as means or agencies of speaking.	**Forms of speech:** the participants share a language although they may have different registers, varieties. The monolingual situation allows for negotiation and clarification.	**Forms of speech:** HI needs to be aware of different registers, varieties, used by both participants. HI shares a language with each although not necessarily the register or variety. There is room for negotiation or clarification with each of the participants. HI's variety and register add another layer of complexity to be considered.
Norms of interaction: rules governing speaking.	**Norms of interaction:** generally participants share the same sense of appropriateness of asking, answering, turn-taking.	**Norms of interaction:** HCP and the non-English speaking P may not share the same sense of appropriateness of ways of speaking. For example, if P is from a Spanish-speaking country, where total overlapping is the sociolinguistic rule during a conversation, and HCP is expecting turn-taking, some tension may arise based on misunderstandings or misconceptions. HI as a third

Table 1 (*cont.*)

Hymes' components of speech	Monolingual communicative event in a hospital setting	Interpreted communicative event in a hospital setting
		participant may sometimes try to be in control of the conversational traffic, adding an extra component to the tension. HI may also decide to educate the parties on this difference and another component is thus added.
Norms of interpreting: the belief system of a community and how that interacts with the frame of references for understanding utterances.	**Norms of interpreting:** generally participants share the same sense of what a hesitation or a lack of eye contact means.	**Norms of interpreting:** generally HI will have a two-way focus on interpreting of utterances. HI is concerned with how to portray the speaker in a way that is acceptable to the listener and vice-versa. If P were Korean, he/she probably would not look HCP in the eye; if HCP is not familiar with Korean culture, he/she will probably be suspicious. HI needs to be alert. Also, HI, as another co-participant, brings another set of norms of interpreting that need to be brokered.
Genres: categories of speech (e.g. poem, myth, tale, proverb, riddle, curse, prayer, oration, lecture); though often coincidental with speech event, genres must be treated as analytically independent.	**Genres:** both participants benefit from recognizing the genre of the speech that does not always coincide with the event. For example, the HCP may lecture the patient over a certain occurrence but certainly the event is not a lecture. The recognition of the genre is the responsibility of the parties, i.e. P and HCP.	**Genres:** HI benefits from recognizing the genre of the speech that does not always coincide with the event. Because the monolingual interlocutors do not have access to the original genre, they depend on HI to recognize it. HI, however, may decide to alter it and therefore causes two genres to co-exist. For example, HCP may be giving part of a sermon to imitate a priest's advice to take good care of the body, but he/she will most definitely not be preaching. Sometimes this difference is not evident to the other participant and HI has to make this explicit. Other times, HI may find this patronizing and alter the genre in his/her rendition.

HCP = healthcare provider HI = hospital interpreter P = patient other hand, in an MCE if speaker and listener do not share the scene, it is up to them to clarify this and negotiate meaning with each other if needed.

- *Participants.* In an ICE, there are three participants in constant interaction with each other. The interpreter brings in roles that cannot be predicted (traffic controller, educator, summarizer, broker, among others). In an MCE, there are two participants, and the interaction is limited to them. An ICE has more participants and more interactions, which add to its complexity.
- *Purposes and outcomes.* Differences in culture and language may affect the outcome of an ICE. Beliefs and expectations may not necessarily be shared. (This is not to imply that this could not be true for the MCE.) The fact that there are three participants instead of two in an ICE adds to the complexity of the interaction, which in turn impacts on the outcomes. The interpreter's participation adds layers of possibilities to the outcome. That is not the case in an MCE.
- *Message form and content.* During the ICE, the interpreters try to discover and explore the competence of speakers with whom they are not familiar. They have the possibility to negotiate the message form and content of the other interlocutors while they interject their own.
- *Forms of speech.* In an ICE, interpreters are working with the speakers' and the listeners' forms of speech, while introducing their own. Language is not shared among the three interlocutors. Only the interpreter has a language in common with the other two. This is not the case in an MCE where both participants share a common language.
- *Norms of interaction and norms of interpretation.* In an MCE, there is a two-way interaction of two parties who, in general, share norms of interaction and interpretation. In this sense, the differences in norms of interaction and interpretation are minimal. Alternatively, in an ICE, both monolingual speakers negotiate rules of interaction and interpretation through the interpreter, whose own set of rules, in turn, adds to the complexity of the interaction. This analysis makes evident the fact that monolingual and interpreted communicative events have more differences than similarities and that these differences are the result of the complexity of the ICE.

The lens of linguistic anthropology shows us how each interlocutor constructs and co-constructs messages by looking at interlocutors who are socially responsible in their talk. "To say that a human being as a social actor, is 'responsible' is a relatively new way of speaking in English," argues Richard Niebhur (1963: 65). "Deriving from an older notion of 'responsiveness,' a quality of participation in dialogue, the newer sense of 'responsibility' that has emerged in the modern era indexes the development of an idea of 'the continuity of a self with a relatively consistent scheme of interpreting of what it is reacting to . . . [and] continuity in the community of agents to which response is being made" (Niebhur 1963: 65). The collection of essays in Hill and Irvine (1992) suggests that participation in dialogue is a sense of responsibility to which attention must be turned. A recent paradigm shift in linguistic anthropology assigns meaning to dialogic constructions in interactive processes rather than to the individual speaker. This paradigm shift is crucial for the study of the interpersonal role of the interpreter. It allows us to see the interpreter as an interlocutor who participates in the dialogue. This participation carries responsibility and it is evident in the talk.

Other bodies of knowledge that also account for this paradigm shift are the ethnography of speaking (focusing on speech event and contextualization of meaning), symbolic interactionism and the sociological study of a conversation, philosophy and literary criticism, and discourse analysis. The paradigm shift that emphasizes dialogicality and social construction of meaning implies a close connection between knowledge and agency (Hill and Irvine 1992). Socially situated participants interact to establish facts and collect or request information by exercising their agency in the construction of knowledge. Their agency is also materialized when they act upon what they have come to know, suspect, or prove. This means that as participants in interactions, individuals are knowledgeable and responsible agents. The key to analyzing the responsibility is in seeing it manifested during interactions rather than in the individual intention of the speaker as suggested by the personalist view of meaning (Duranti 1992).

In a case study of a Samoan village, Duranti (1992) illustrates the ways in which the speakers' responsibility is contextually and cooperatively defined. Meaning should not be conceived as being owned by an individual, but rather seen as a result of cooperative achievement. This concept of meaning is especially interesting when compared to that present in the literature on interpreting, which claims that meaning is objective and independent of the parties who utter the words. Based on the ideology of an objective meaning, the field argues for an invisible language switcher that can communicate the same meaning in a different language. The lens of linguistic anthropology helps us understand how this conception can be a fallacy. This lens also allows us to examine the complexity of the interaction of the interlocutors and the co-construction of meaning as they speak.

Another example of social co-construction of meaning and responsibility emerges from Irvine's study of insult and responsibility in a Wolof village. She argues that insults are not simply a set of statements, but instead "a communicative effect constructed in interaction, constructed out of the interplay of linguistic and social features, where the propositional context of an utterance is only one such feature. In fact, the content could even look like a compliment, were it examined in isolation" (1992: 110). Irvine uses the example of a praise singer that was hired to sing praises of a family of the leatherworker caste. Because he thought he was not fairly paid for his services, the singer ridiculed this family by over-praising them. The listeners became aware of this as the singer called the family's ancestors kings and queens (which they were obviously not), thus turning the praise into an insult. This example is a good illustration of Irvine's point of social responsibility. On the one hand, the family could not object to being over-praised, because no overt or direct insult was committed. On the other hand, since the audience knew that many of the praises were done in a sarcastic manner, the family's honor and reputation were tainted. The insult only became an insult for that Wolof family once there was an audience present. This example illustrates how the lens of linguistic anthropology allows us to see the interpreter as someone who, like the other co-participants in the interaction, constructs a message out of the interplay of linguistic and social features and not just out of propositional context that exists independently of the interlocutors.

A further example of co-construction of responsibility and agency is the analysis of Mrs. Patricio's trouble by Hill and Zepeda (1992). Mrs. Patricio's child has been missing school, and Mrs. Patricio does not want this to reflect poorly on her. When she speaks with the principal, Mrs. Patricio seeks to gain her sympathy. Hill and Zepeda's analysis demonstrates that when speakers (of whom Mrs. Patricio constitutes the central example) give accounts of personal experiences, they attempt to construct favorable presentations of the self and to mitigate those representations that might damage the portrayed self. "In doing so," the authors remind us that "they [speakers] reveal everyday cultural frames through which agency and responsibility are understood" (1992: 197). By using rhetorical devices, Mrs. Patricio limits the possibilities of being held personally responsible for the truancy of her son. These rhetorical devices help her distribute the responsibility, thus making responsibility a shared element in a social field rather than the burden of a single agent. Mrs. Patricio achieves this distribution of responsibility by using reported speech, inviting her interlocutor to draw conclusions rather than making explicit statements, and portraying herself as unable to change the course of events based on her legal status and lack of knowledge of the educational system. Through the example of Mrs. Patricio, Hill and Zepeda show how responsibility is neither external to the discourse nor inherent to only one agent; it is shared and co-constructed by the interlocutors.

At the beginning of this chapter Wittgenstein warned us about "even the hugest telescope having an eye-piece no larger than the eye." I have suggested the use of three telescopes to look at the problem of the role of the interpreter. The lenses of sociological and social theories and the one used in linguistic anthropology should not be considered separately, but instead should be utilized collectively as a set of tools whose use can enhance our perspective of the role of the interpreter.

The interplay of these theories conceives an interlocutor that brings to the interaction a set of dispositions, perceptions, and beliefs. This human being exercises agency and responsibility as he/she interacts within an institution that is part of a society. The forces at play in the institution and the society impact on the interaction. Each individual who interacts with other parties becomes a key player in the co-construction of meaning. In doing so, each juggles the impact of both the institution and the society where the interaction is embedded. The interpreter, as a human being, is no exception.

4   California Hope: a public hospital in changing times

> To encompass in research the process of a given thing's development in all its
> phases and changes – from birth to death – fundamentally means to discover
> its nature, its essence, for "it is only in movement that a body shows what it is."
> Thus, the historical study of behavior is not an auxiliary aspect of theoretical
> study, but rather forms its very base.
>
> Lev Vygotsky, *Mind in Society* (1978: 64–5)

Understanding the complexities of medical interpreting and the different roles
interpreters play requires contextualized study of naturalistic data over an
extended period of time. This chapter will describe how these topics are explored
through an ethnography performed in a public hospital. The first part of the chapter will explain the reasons for choosing a medical setting over any other. Next,
the process of obtaining consent will be described. Then, the study itself will
be presented, beginning with a brief description of the city in which the site is
found, the site at large (California Hope), and the informants at the specific site
(the interpreters at Interpreting Services).

Finding a study site

In choosing a site, the next logical step was to look for one in which access
to a wide array of interpreted medical interactions would be available. In this
sense, California Hope (CH)[1] emerged as a unique site, since the number of
ICEs (both face-to-face and over-the-speakerphone) carried out per day at CH
is astonishingly high.[2]

The pilot study

In order to determine feasibility, I conducted a one-year pilot study at CH.
This study involved observation and shadowing of interpreters as well as

---

[1] In order to protect the privacy of participants, the names of all persons, locations, and institutions
are fictitious.
[2] Reference omitted to protect the identity of the site.

note-taking and subsequent analysis of notes. The results of the pilot study evidenced various degrees of visibility of the interpreter during the interaction, confirming CH as a desirable site for observing the interpreter's role.

Once the protocol was deemed feasible, the plan of study was presented to the CH board of directors for approval. Since the nature and theme of this study were different from those usually reviewed by the CH board (e.g. clinical trials for new therapies), and since most board members were either hospital administrators or physicians who interact daily with patients via interpreters, this particular study generated considerable interest among them.

Obtaining consent

After the hospital board had approved the research plan, the managers of all participating departments were provided with copies of consent forms and all other documentation (prospectus and oral consent script to be used with speakerphones). I then set out to meet the participants of the study, either by personal introduction or via e-mail.

CH's Interpreting Service (IS) manager allowed me to meet with each interpreter individually, in order to explain the protocol. These individual meetings were necessary, because it was not feasible to gather all of the interpreters together for a meeting during working hours. The goal of these meetings was not only to describe the study, but also to address (before initiating the study) any concerns that the interpreters might have about the protocol. Two main obstacles emerged at this initial stage of the trust-building process with the interpreters. First, when interpreters are being observed, they immediately suspect that any recordings and observations are made to document the accuracy or lack thereof in their work. Since no one had ever recorded this group of interpreters, they had concerns about the use of the data. Second, the manager insisted on introducing me as an experienced professional and teacher in the field of translation and interpreting, rather than as a researcher collecting data and learning. Despite my attempts to explain my concern about issues of credibility and threat (which were already implanted in the minds of the interpreters), the manager remained firm in his position.

Patient consent was solicited at the beginning of each ICE. Although HCPs had been briefed on the nature of the research and its implementation, they took several months to adjust to the request for consent, each time they called for an interpreter. During face-to-face interpretations, I assumed the responsibility of soliciting consent. During speakerphone interpretations, obtaining consent was the job of the interpreters, which added anywhere from forty-five seconds to two minutes (if participants asked questions) of extra work to each interpreting session.

The in-depth study

The town

Founded in the mid-1700s and incorporated in the mid-1800s, Conte is at present ranked among the ten largest cities in the state and the country[3] (Jan.1, 2001 State Department of Finance). At the heart of this dynamic region is a flourishing economy sustained in part by many high-tech and manufacturing companies. The Conte metropolitan area ranks among the first ten national leaders in exports, possessing strong economic ties with countries throughout the world. In terms of household income, Conte is ranked among the top five cities in the US, based on a median household annual income of approximately $50,000.00. The city is committed to its mission of delivering the highest quality services in the most cost-effective manner. The annual budget is in excess of one billion dollars, making it possible for the city to offer a full range of services to its residents and businesses. Its educational services include seven universities and colleges and eleven school districts.

Conte takes pride in the cultural and ethnic diversity of its population and workforce and the rich cultural identity of its many neighborhoods; residents speak more than forty-six different languages (Unified School District). The population, which currently exceeds 800,000, is composed of African Americans (4.4 percent), Asian or Pacific Islanders (18.6 percent), Hispanics (26.6 percent), Whites (49.6 percent), and Others (0.8 percent).

The hospital

At the edge of Conte lies California Hope, a public hospital owned and operated by the County of Velazquez. CH was built in 1876 on its present site through the efforts of Dr. Goodheart, Velazquez's first medical practitioner. The hospital's first training program, a school of nursing (with three students) was established in 1905. The Pediatric Unit was constructed in 1914, followed by many other specialty units. By 1952, CH became one of the first hospitals in the nation to be accredited by the Joint Commission for the Accreditation of Hospitals. The first university-affiliated residency program was established in 1959, in conjunction with a prestigious West Coast school. The addition of departments and clinics culminated in 1990, when the west wing opened with a new intensive care unit, transitional care unit, and maternity and primary care units.

Like any other public hospital in the country, CH struggles for funds necessary for renovations and upgrades of its facilities. At present, CH stretches along

---

[3] Figures have been rounded to protect the identity of the site and they reflect the situation at the time of the study.

several city blocks, and consists of eight clinics and two large buildings: the old and new wings of the hospital. Specialty clinics offer services in women and children's health, diabetes, nutrition, prenatal care, rehabilitation services, tuberculosis, and AIDS care and education. Informational pamphlets are offered in English, Spanish, and Vietnamese in each of these clinics.

Since 1876, CH has forged a tradition of service and dedication to the health of the Conte community. Each year has witnessed a growth in the demand for its services. The staff at CH cares for thousands of hospitalized patients and provides one-half million out-patient and emergency consults annually. CH is affiliated with six teaching institutions throughout Northern California, but it also enjoys a fine reputation for its own freestanding medical education programs.

CH has established a strong foundation as the Conte community's principal healthcare provider. It is the only hospital in the county with an open-door policy that guarantees access to needed medical care, regardless of ability to pay. As the hospital's mission states, it is "dedicated to the health of the whole community."

In addition to a high level of basic service provided by fourteen departments, CH also provides sophisticated medical specialty services. These include a rehabilitation program (ranked as one of the best in the US for spinal cord and head injuries), a regional burn center, a trauma center, and a neonatal intensive care unit. The hospital also offers CHConnections, which is a medical advice and appointments hotline, available at no cost to members of the California Hope Family Health Plan (CHFHP). Through this service, specially trained staff members guide the caller in scheduling a medical visit or going to the emergency room, depending upon the nature of the patient's illness or injury. The CHConnections hotline is available twenty-four hours a day, seven days a week and appointments can be scheduled Monday through Friday from 8:00 a.m. to 9:30 p.m. and Saturday and Sunday from 8:00 a.m. to 5:00 p.m. Interpreting services are available for non-English speaking healthplan members.

CH's mission statement declares that it provides a user-friendly physical environment with safe, clean, inviting and accessible facilities, and that employees and volunteers should have the equipment and supplies needed to support their work. The mission statement also sets forth patients as the first priority. It reads, "We uphold the dignity of our patients and treat them with respect and compassion." During my time at CH, I witnessed some evidence of that priority in action. However, meeting the needs of such a diverse population is not always an easy task. The community that utilizes the services of CH reflects Conte's diverse ethnic and socio-economic pool of residents. The population served by CH ranges from middle class to working class, but the average patient is sub-working class. Most of the patients are African American, Asian, and Hispanic. The Hispanic patient population constitutes the largest group served by IS.

The study site

CH's department of IS was chosen as the study site because of its uniqueness in providing a place to observe and study the role of the interpreter in instances of cross-cultural communication. There were a number of features which made CH a desirable study site. Out of the medical institutions offering a full-fledged interpreting service (such as UCLA, Stanford, Santa Clara Valley Medical, Rochester, Mayo, Seattle, and Massachusetts Medical Center), CH was among the first to provide face-to-face and over-the-speakerphone interpreting on site through IS. Additionally, CH has the highest productivity in terms of interpreting per hour and day. Finally, CH has the largest staff of Spanish medical interpreters, which was the linguistic combination of interest to this study.

On-site telephonic interpreting is conducted through speakerphones. When a non-English-speaking patient walks into a room, the HCP calls IS and an interpreter comes on the line. This initiates a three-party conversation in which two parties (patient and HCP) are in the same room, and the third party (the interpreter) is present through a speakerphone. Calls made from different clinics and areas of the hospital come into IS through a central computerized system. Calls for face-to-face interpreting are channeled through a dispatcher who assigns interpreters, either according to availability or other special requests.[4] Requests for speakerphone interpreting are received by an automated system, which dispatches calls to available interpreters.

At a remote on-campus site, interpreters answer calls in the order in which they were received. CH medical and auxiliary staff members are trained in the use of remote (i.e. non face-to-face) interpreters. This training is based on a set of written guidelines provided by the IS manager. Oftentimes, both HCP and patient must compensate for the interpreter's physical absence by making over-explicit statements. For example, if patients point to some part of their body in response to a question, HCPs must relay that fact to interpreters. Therefore, in essence, while the interpreter acts as the voice for both healthcare provider and patient, these two parties may also act as the eyes of the interpreter.

The staff

The interpreting force at IS consists of ten full-time and three part-time Spanish interpreters. There are also two full-time Chinese (Mandarin and Cantonese), two Vietnamese interpreters, and one part-time Russian interpreter.

When the work capacity has reached its maximum, IS draws from the bilingual employees of CH and from commercial companies providing over-the-telephone interpreting for the communicative needs of patients. Whenever there

---

[4] For example, special requests are sometimes made on the basis of gender.

is a request for interpreting and all interpreters are already on assignment, or there is a need for a language other than those covered by IS, the dispatcher (who answers the phone request) locates an IS-certified bilingual employee within the hospital do the interpreting. If unable to locate a CH-certified bilingual employee, the dispatcher must then call the telephone-interpreting company.[5]

Of the ten full-time Spanish interpreters, nine are on duty between 8:30 a.m. and 5:00 p.m., and one is on duty between 1:00 p.m. and 9:00 p.m. Certain days of the week and times of the day are busier than others; the two part-time staff members are called when needed. During my twenty-two months of observation, there was always a part-time Spanish interpreter at IS.

The IS department manager at CH holds a Master's degree in foreign languages and has twenty-two years of experience in medical interpreting. He is responsible for hiring interpreters. For that purpose, he designed a test of medical vocabulary, interpreting skills, and memory retention in both directions (English into Spanish and Spanish into English). The test progresses from short phrases into complex paragraphs. During test taking, candidates may ask for repetition, but they may not take notes. There are no guidelines for administering the test, nor is there data available on its validity or reliability.

Several bilingual candidates are tested on a monthly basis from within and outside CH. If they pass the test, CH employees become certified and are called upon to interpret if needed. For that, they receive a monthly bonus of sixty dollars. Non-CH employees, if certified, are hired on a part-time basis unless there is a need for a full-time position, which is then advertised in the county office. During my time at CH, a position was opened in February 2000 and was still not filled in June of that same year. During that time, two of the ten participants of this study worked as part-time interpreters.

Table 2 illustrates the interpreters' demographic data. Interpreters at CH must meet the following requirements: (1) two years of experience in the field (as medical interpreter, translator, or bilingual medical assistant); (2) bilingual ability; and (3) passing the IS test. All of the interpreters are native Spanish speakers, except for one (Annette). The ratio of females to males is four to six, with an average age of forty-six years. Although none of the interpreters has actually received formal education in translation or interpreting, each has field-related experience. The background of the CH Spanish-language interpreters varies widely, from high school graduate to physician. Seniority does not necessarily correspond with age, nor does it correspond with extent of formal education. For example, Vicente, who has fifteen years of experience and is the oldest CH interpreter, has a medical school diploma from Rumania. However Consuelo, who has second-highest seniority (twelve years), has a high school

---

[5] Linguistic resources are limited at CH. Due to the high prices charged by telephone interpreting companies, these services are only solicited when absolutely necessary.

Table 2 *California Hope interpreters' demographic data*

Informants	Age	Seniority (years) coded/ EH	Education	Job-related experience	Ethnic background***
Julio	34	5 – coded	High school	Pediatric Unit assistant	Mexico / Mexican American
Annette	45	6 months – EH	Associate of Science	Court interpreter	USA / American
Consuelo	52	12 – coded	High school	Bilingual employee	Guatemala / Hispanic
Marcos	48	4 – coded	Bachelor's degree Engineering	International consultant/engineer	Chile / Chilean American
Vicente	60	15 – coded	Medical school	Doctor in Rumania	Peru/Rumania / Peruvian/Rumanian American
Elda	55	13 – coded	BA	ER interpreter	Mexico / Mexican American
Joaquín	35	9 – coded	High school	Medical translator	Mexico / Mexican
Mariana	48	8 – coded	MA	Teacher	Mexico / Mexican American
Mauro	50	8 – coded	Medical school	Physician in Mexico	Mexico / Mexican American
Rogelio	33	2 – EH	Medical school	Physician in Mexico	Mexico / Mexican American

Notes: * Coded refers to full-time employment condition. Coded employees receive benefits.
** EH (Extra-help) refers to part-time work. Extra-help individuals do not receive benefits.
*** In this category, line 1 refers to where interpreters were born and educated; line 2 refers to the term used by them in their self-identification.

education. Joaquín, whose formal education ends at the high school level, has nine years of experience as a CH interpreter, while Rogelio, who is the youngest interpreter and has worked at IS for only two years, has a Medical Degree from Mexico. Annette, who has six months of experience at CH, has an Associate of Science degree. And Marcos is an engineer!

Therefore, like most medical interpreters, the interpreters working at CH have not received formal education in medical interpreting. This is consistent with the reality of the field, where opportunities to learn the tricks of the trade do not abound. At the time I was conducting the study, there were not many choices available to interpreters who wanted to specialize in the medical setting or to bilinguals who wanted to explore becoming a medical interpreter. Medical interpreting was a trade that was learned by doing: first by shadowing others and then by practicing under the wing of those more experienced. At CH, the novice interpreters shadowed the more experienced interpreters for a certain period of time. In fact, that is how I collected data for this study (following interpreters and interpreters in training).

If one of the CH interpreters decided to pursue options in continuing education (when available) it would be difficult to do, especially for the full-time interpreters whose schedule does not accommodate opportunities for professional development. All continuing education or professional advancement must be done in the interpreters' own time and at their own expense. Additionally, under the current system of remuneration, professional improvement does not result in a salary increase or better working conditions. Thus, interpreters really have no motivation to pursue continuing education, other than their personal desire to improve.

Most of the interpreters live near CH, with the exception of one person, whose commute is over an hour. She is a single mother of five children and cannot afford housing in the area. All of the other interpreters are homeowners. Most of them have families, some with grown children, and others with young children.

The group of interpreters has been together for a long time. Some have been co-workers for over ten years. This may explain the sense of family that I got when I first entered IS. The atmosphere is extremely warm and friendly. A well-developed camaraderie is evident to any observer; they inquire about each other's family members, and they cover for each other in case of need. For example, if an interpreter who is feeling fatigued receives a face-to-face assignment on the other side of the hospital grounds, another interpreter may volunteer to take his/his her place. Interpreters ask each other for help with unfamiliar terms or concepts, sharing linguistic resources. They also work together to create a light-hearted atmosphere in their stressful working environment. Interpreters can often be seen teasing one another, shaking the chair of a colleague during a phone interpretation, tying together the sleeves of a colleague's blazer left hanging on a chair or launching wadded-up paper messages over the cubicle dividers.

As in any family, they celebrate one another's birthdays. They have their own special way of honoring the person whose birthday is being celebrated. Elda is the treasurer of the group. She collects money from her colleagues and is in charge of buying the birthday cake, gift, and card. All of the interpreters secretly sign the card, and those who are available (i.e. not on an interpreting assignment) quickly deliver the gift, card, and cake to the guest of honor's cubicle. The birthday celebrant receives happy birthday wishes coming from cubicles in all directions, and cake is distributed throughout the work area, as interpreters continue to answer calls without missing a beat.

The manager also receives a card, cake, and gift on his birthday and con-tributes towards those of the others, but since the vertical hierarchy is in place he is not part of the inner circle. The manager supervises the work, schedules holidays and emergency room rotations, and edits the translations. He is also in charge of training and of writing some guidelines for the staff at CH. When interpreting needs are at a peak, he also interprets into and from Spanish. But generally, most of his time is spent compiling statistics for IS and monitor-ing his team of interpreters through the automated call-distribution software installed on his computer. This navigation system allows the manager to open different screens for language groups and to see who is doing face-to-face or over-the-speakerphone interpreting, who is translating, and who is on a lunch or restroom break. The navigation system works with the codes that interpreters enter. If one interpreter forgets to enter a code and is away from the phone, the manager notices this immediately and goes to that interpreter's cubicle to investigate. The manager has little tolerance for this type of irregularity, and the interpreters know it.

The workplace

IS shares its workplace (a trailer) with medical admitting clerks and nurses. The trailer, which has different areas, cubicles, and offices, is a short walk from the entrance of the main hospital, across the visitor parking lot. The only office in the interpreters' workspace is that of the manager. The other IS staff members occupy open cubicle spaces. Interpreters sit in cubicles that are three panels wide. All cubicles are alike, except for those at the end of each row, which are given to the most senior interpreters. These cubicles have one window and two panels. Two of the panels sustain tables that create an L-shaped work area. Each cubicle contains a telephone. Some interpreters have personalized their cubicles with family pictures, mirrors, or posters. Job-related information is posted on the dividing walls of most cubicles, along with lunch schedules, emergency room rotation schedules, holiday coverage plans, and commonly used phone numbers (such as the directory of certified bilingual employees and directory of clinics). In almost every Spanish interpreter's cubicle, a magazine rack houses English–Spanish medical dictionaries and glossaries and bilingual references.

Some interpreters have added more of a personal touch to their cubicles than others, and this can be the subject of the others' amusement. For example, Joaquín teases Annette for having a lot of statuettes of saints in her cubicle, for believing in palm reading, and for hanging what he considers to be weird stuff on her cubicle walls. Annette's cubicle is tidy. She has a magazine rack on one wall, where she keeps the following books: *Mastering Spanish Vocabulary*, *Quick Medical Terminology*, *A Usage Guide to Spanish Grammar and Idioms*, and *Roger Medical Dictionary English/Spanish*. There are also three plants, one stuffed toy dog, photos of her five children and her parents, and two framed certificate degrees (Paralegal and Associate of Science). There is also a water cooler. All photocopies of information containing phone extensions and codes are preserved in plastic sheets and hang against the wall with thumbtacks. There is a small mirror hanging in one corner, a Bible calendar, and a stand with prayers for the day. At any given time during the workday, warm water and Dr. Pepper can be found on Annette's desk. According to Annette, these drinks help to keep her throat moist and preserve her voice.

Another less personalized but well-organized cubicle is that of Elda. There are three magazine racks to the left of the computer (as is the case in all cubicles). The racks contain two plants and bottles of drinking water. Posted on one of the side panels are a calendar and an emergency department rotation schedule, while photos of Elda's family and co-workers grace the central panel. There are several birthday cards on the desk. Elda keeps a running list of gifts to purchase and cards to be signed. There is also a calculator, a pencil holder, two staplers, sunglasses, nail enamel, hand lotion, a coffee mug, and a scotch tape dispenser on Elda's desk.

The layout of Interpreting Services is shown in figure 5.

The amenities provided for those working in the trailer include two individual restrooms, two double restrooms, and a cubicle where soft drinks and snacks are sold. There is also a dining area which houses four tables and twenty-two chairs, two refrigerators, two microwave ovens, a coffee maker, and a water dispenser. Employees are charged for water and coffee. The dining area is also used for union meetings and potluck lunches (e.g. baby showers or retirement parties), usually by medical admitting clerks and nurses. The interpreters rarely participate in such events, since their working schedule does not permit it.

Working hours and interpreters' responsibilities

At IS, interpreters sign in at 8:30 a.m. and sign out at 5:00 p.m. They are allowed two fifteen-minute breaks (one in the morning and one in the afternoon) and a

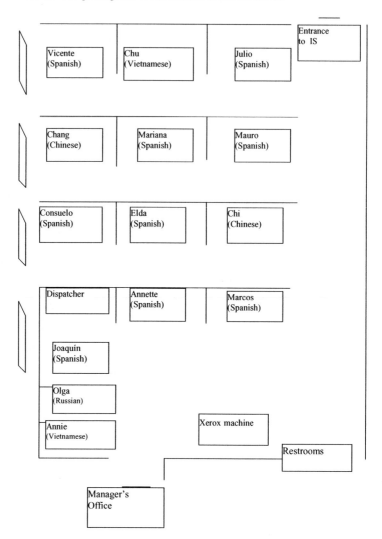

Figure 5   Interpreting services floor plan

thirty-minute lunch break. There is a schedule for lunch breaks since a certain number of interpreters must be available at all times. One interpreter is expected to begin a lunch break every ten minutes between 11:45 a.m. and 1:15 p.m. Interpreters are not allowed to take their fifteen-minute breaks within forty-five minutes prior to or after the lunch period. They are permitted to be away from their phones for various reasons (face-to-face interpreting, restroom, translation assignment, training session, or staff meeting), but before leaving their cubicles, they must sign out with the appropriate code. The computer system keeps track of the time spent in those activities according to the codes entered. Each time interpreters leave for a face-to-face assignment, they must return to the trailer, sign in, and do at least one more task before taking a break. If an interpreter fails to follow this protocol, the computer system automatically includes the break time in the length of the face-to-face assignment, which causes a discrepancy between the computer system's log and the interpreter's log.

Interpreters are required to complete a daily log of their interpretation tasks. The log includes the following information: HCP's name, site of origin of the call, patient's name, patient's medical record number, reason for calling, starting and ending times of interpreting, and length of the interpretation. Each day, interpreters must add up the number of interpretations performed and the minutes they spent interpreting. At the end of each week, interpreters submit a summary of the week's activities to the IS manager. These data normally coincide with those recorded by the system. In case of discrepancy, the manager calls the interpreter in question to discuss the inconsistency. These data are vital for the manager's productivity report. Throughout the duration of this study, a peak day for one interpreter consisted of sixty requests for interpreting.

A typical day at Interpreting Services

At 8:00 a.m., the visitor's parking lot is empty. It is a short walk from the trailer that houses Interpreting Services. Activity within the trailer can be seen as early as 8:00 a.m., but IS begins its daily service to the public at 8:30 a.m. Roberto, the manager, arrives minutes before 8:15 a.m., as does the dispatcher. Generally, interpreters arrive a few minutes before 8:30 a.m. Some stop by the dining room and leave lunch boxes in the refrigerators. Others leave lunch boxes in their cubicles. They sign onto the system and are ready for the first call at 8:30 a.m. While waiting for calls, some interpreters read the newspaper or prepare their logs, and others discuss current events or their previous evening's activities. Generally, conversations occur between neighboring cubicles, although it is not unusual to hear conversations across rows of cubicles.

Interpreters begin taking morning breaks at 10:00 a.m. They generally use breaks to go to the hospital cafeteria for coffee, to make phone calls, or to pay bills, except for Consuelo who eats her lunch during her morning break at 10:30 a.m. so that she can walk during her thirty-minute lunch break. (Other interpreters have tried to follow Consuelo's fitness example, but have found it difficult to maintain the discipline.) All morning breaks must be taken an hour before the first lunch begins.

At 11:45 a.m., interpreters begin taking thirty-minute lunch breaks. They follow the schedule, occasionally switching break times with one another when the need arises. For example, sometimes interpreters are detained with face-to-face interpreting at their lunch break time. In this case, other interpreters switch lunch times with them. The maximum time overlap that any two interpreters have during the lunch break is twenty minutes. Sometimes, Rogelio and Elda use this time to walk together.

Once the last lunch break is over, interpreters are required to wait one hour before they can take an afternoon break. Mornings are generally busier than afternoons, although this is not necessarily the case on a Monday afternoon or following a holiday. Monday and Tuesday are the busiest days of the week, and Friday is generally the slowest, but this may vary by season and time of year. For example, during this observation period, the busiest days occurred during the flu season and on the Fourth of July.

Interpreters know no down time. If there is not a high need for interpreting on a given day, there is always translation work that was due several days ago. The translated material utilized by CH varies from educational pamphlets on nutrition and diabetes (food pyramids, insulin log) to how a patient can prepare for a computed tomography (CT) scan. Some of the texts are concrete and self-explanatory. Other texts vary in the complexity of cultural adaptation and unit conversion, or research for acronyms. If interpreters find the comprehension of a text to be hindered by awkwardness in the source language, they call the CH press office for clarification. When the original text authors are available and approachable, the clarification is usually quick and requires little effort. Other times, the original author is unavailable, and the interpreter speaks with someone who is unable to explain what another writer has produced. This is a source of great frustration for the interpreters, who always seem to be pressed for time.

Translation and interpreting call for some of the same skills and strategies (such as ability to convey meaning in a different language and ability to render an idea in a culturally acceptable form). Although they are similar in many respects, these two disciplines call for very different aptitudes and skills on the part of the performer. The translator seeks out the best suitable equivalence for a given text, working on the style and context within a given period of time, thus becoming a co-author of the text. The interpreter, on the other hand, is required to produce an adequate conversational equivalence under the pressure of time, thus becoming a co-speaker in the interaction. Interpreters at CH switch back and forth between translating and interpreting. On some days, they are assigned only translation jobs, permitting them to temporarily shelve their interpreters' hats. On other days, when requests for interpreting are sparse, they perform both functions. This results in a translator at work whose task is often interrupted to attend an interpreting assignment, a situation to which interpreters at CH have not only adapted, but have also mastered.

Adding even more to the complexity of their job, interpreters must switch between over-the-speakerphone and face-to-face interpreting, and they cover a dispatcher rotation once a week. Just as translating and interpreting call for different skills, so do speakerphone and face-to-face interpreting. Although both modes of interpreting can be stressful, their stressors are different. In the case of face-to-face interpreting, the interpreter must cope with the stress of being physically present with the other parties (eye contact, emotional presence, physical presence). Speakerphone interpreters lack the eye contact between interpreter and other parties, but this does not mean that they are emotionally absent from the situation. In addition, each speakerphone interpreting session requires constant compensatory clarification statements, which can raise the stress level for the interpreter. Since no two days are alike, there is neither opportunity for boredom nor complacency at IS. In spite of the fact that no two hours are even alike, the IS interpreters face these challenges with passion and calm, as if they were part of an ordinary routine.

As Vygotsky reminds us at the opening of this chapter, "to encompass in research the process of a given thing's development in all its phases and changes means to discover its nature, its essence, for 'it is only in movement that a body shows what it is.'" We have now explored the nature of the interpreter's job, watching it unfold itself through its own movement. Throughout the course of the job, the interpreter's interpersonal role manifests itself. In the next chapter, we organize how we capture the movement as we get ready to look at those manifestations.

5   Putting it all together

During my stay at CH, I spent a lot of time with the informants, asking questions, observing, shadowing them, and taking notes on what they do and say. While doing this, I continuously followed "hunches – which we could call hypotheses – that helped [me] figure out why things happen as they do" (LeCompte and Schensul 1999:11). The recursive nature of questioning, obtaining answers, refining questions, getting more detailed answers, and searching for ways to corroborate, negate, clarify, or expand original formulations allowed me to reorganize my sense of what was happening at CH. In doing this, I paid close attention to negative evidence, i.e. behaviors, instances, or other facts that appeared to disconfirm the construct of a visible interpreter that I had already found. This was especially important, in order to avoid the temptation of dismissing these facts as anomalies. Instances when interpreters would step out of role and argue with providers on behalf of the patient were difficult to discern, and the process was time consuming. However, they were worth it, because they helped me refine and modify my search (Miles and Huberman 1984).

This recursive analysis started as soon as I entered CH and continued for three years. It was guided by copious inscriptions (head notes), descriptions (field notes that turned into conceptual memos for myself), and transcriptions. Throughout the course of my fieldwork, I tried to remain conscious of any biases about the field of interpreting that I might harbor. It was also important for me to keep mindful of any biases that I might have had about the medical setting as well. Growing up in a home with two scientists for parents (my mother, a biochemist and pharmacologist, and my father, a physician), I spent a large portion of my childhood hanging around laboratories and hospitals. Since dinner conversations usually revolved around the day's happenings, medical jargon and technical terms became a regular part of my vocabulary. During the collection of data, I often reminded myself to write notes about occurrences at the hospital that might have seemed commonplace to me, and not simply regard them as normal, but rather, as something of ethnographic interest to this study. In the next sections, I present the procedures used in the collection, coding, and analysis of the data.

Data collection, coding, and analysis

Twenty-two months of observations at CH resulted in a corpus of ICEs (audio recording of face-to-face and over-the-speakerphone interpreted sessions), observation notes, and semi-structured interviews with interpreters and manager, artifacts, and interpreter interpersonal role inventory (IPRI) surveys.

In making sense of the interpreter's role, my study and analyses of the corpus were directed by triangulation. In the following sections, I explain how the different sources of data were composed and contrasted, coded, and analyzed to enrich the perspective I gained on the interpreters' role at CH.

Artifacts

Table 3 lists the artifacts collected at CH during the period of observation and the manner in which they were analyzed.

Collecting artifacts was part of my routine at Interpreting Services. I visited several offices on campus (e.g. the Office of Patient Services) to obtain realia that would represent CH as a whole entity. For example, I obtained from the transportation office a list of the bus, train, and shuttle schedules for the lines that serve CH, because the modes of transportation used by patients could speak about the social aspects of that population.

The IS manager provided me with various guidelines, pamphlets, and translation samples. He also shared with me the IS candidates' exam, which measures medical vocabulary, interpretation skills, and memory retention in both directions, progressing from short phrases into complex paragraphs.[1] In order to be considered for employment, a candidate must pass this test.

I also observed the interpreters' unique system for sending messages (which were also coded as artifacts). A *message* is a handwritten note on a wadded-up piece of paper. Sending a message consists of tossing the paper ball over the cubicle dividers into the cubicle of the person whom they are trying to reach. They consider it to be an effective means of communicating with one another without disrupting the work of others. Glitches in this system only arise when a message lands in someone's coffee. Most messages (which are only sent when the manager is out of the office) pertain to parts of an interpreting session that the sender can overhear from his workspace. However, they can also include personal or work-related questions, or simply plans to take a walk in the lunch break.

Field notes

The collection and use of field notes is summarized in table 4.

---

[1] In order to protect IS test confidentiality, I am unable to reproduce the test in its entirety.

Table 3 *Artifacts*

Collection	Coding and analysis
• From IS manager: medical translator guidelines and guidelines for interpreting sessions at CH; sample of entry test; sample of written materials that interpreters must translate; sample of translations made by currently employed interpreters; sample of corrections made by manager; samples of publications about IS at CH (*NY Times, CHIA Newsletter*) • From interpreters: samples of messages passed among interpreters during work hours; samples of messages sent by manager to interpreters; photos of interpreters and their families • From various offices on the CH campus: samples of pamphlets handed out to patients at CH (English and Spanish); data on hospital statistics; hospital maps; transportation schedules • Miscellaneous: county-wide advertisement for interpreter/translator position at CH; photographs of CH and IS; city maps	• Artifacts were analyzed for content. They were contrasted with one another and with other forms of data. For example, interpreters' messages to one another were contrasted with field notes and observations on informant's interaction and camaraderie, or the contents of the CH interpreter certification test were compared to the interview with the IS manager on the expected qualifications.

Table 4 *Field notes*

Collection	Coding and analysis
• Mostly narrative or descriptive, but sometimes included verbatim comments by informants. • Notes were taken during several informal individual interviews with the interpreters and the IS manager. • Notes were taken during the recorded interpreting sessions (face-to-face and speakerphone), as well as during the semi-structured interviews. • In one psychiatric consult, I was permitted to take notes but not to make an audio recording.	• Notes were transcribed into computer files. Comments and preliminary analyses were added. • Notes were then organized into chronological files, which were eventually organized into topical files. • Notes were analyzed for content and compared to recordings of ICEs and interviews on role. For example, when interpreters referred to themselves as patient comforters, I sought out evidence of behaviors that illustrated that role during recorded ICEs.

In addition to audio recordings, handwritten field notes were taken each day. The purpose of these narrative or descriptive notes was to supplement the audio recordings and to capture in writing everything that I was unable to tape. In one case, during a hearing between a psychiatric patient and a staff member in front of a court officer in which no audio recording was permitted, I was only able to take handwritten notes. At the end of each observation day, I routinely transcribed the field notes into computer files. In doing so, I also wrote notes, comments, and a preliminary analysis between slash bars to separate them from the actual data. Field notes were organized into chronological files and then into topical files, which were analyzed for content and compared to interviews on role and recordings of ICEs.

The interpreter interpersonal role inventory

The interpreter interpersonal role inventory (IPRI) was originally constructed as part of my doctoral studies, which examined interpreters' behaviors in their practice and their beliefs about their role in a cross-cultural communication event across settings (i.e. in the courts, in conferences, in hospitals, or in government agencies) (Angelelli 2001 and 2003). The IPRI includes demographic information and thirty-eight items which measure the variable visibility with its five subcomponents: (1) alignment with the parties; (2) establishing trust with and facilitating mutual respect between the parties; (3) communicating affect as well as message; (4) explaining cultural gaps, and interpreting culture as well as language; and (5) establishing communication rules during the conversation. A summary of the use of the IPRI is given in table 5.

Each of the ten Spanish/English interpreters who participated in the study was asked to complete an IPRI. Administering the IPRI was relatively simple, since the interpreters could complete it in their own time. Some interpreters filled it out while having lunch or waiting for assignments. Others took it home and returned it after a couple of days. The manager and other interpreters working at IS who did not participate in the study (three Vietnamese and one Russian) also completed an IPRI. All IPRIs were completed and returned, with the exception of one Spanish interpreter who misplaced it and never completed a second one. The responses of the IPRIs were entered into a Statistical Package for the Social Sciences (SPSS) file and analyzed together with 293 more cases that participated in the larger study (Angelelli 2001 and 2003). In the end, the IPRI proved to be a valid and reliable instrument designed to investigate interpreters' perceptions of their role and the visibility of the interpreter. The completed surveys were triangulated with observation notes and interviews.

Table 5 *Interpreter interpersonal role inventory*

Collection	Coding and analysis
• Fourteen interpreters and the IS manager were asked to complete the IPRI. • Of those given an IPRI, only one person did not complete and return it. • The IPRI was designed to measure interpreters' perceptions of their role and to investigate invisibility, which was defined by the following behaviors: 1. alignment with one of the parties 2. establishment of trust or facilitation of mutual respect 3. communication of affect and message 4. interpreting culture and language (by explaining cultural gaps) 5. establishment of communication rules during the conversation	• Completed surveys were triangulated with observation notes and interviews. • Responses were entered into an SPSS file for statistical analyses. • Descriptive analyses were performed for the demographic data. Gender, age and personal identification with more dominant or less dominant groups were correlated with the dependent variable visibility.

Table 6 *Interviews*

Collection	Coding and analysis
• All ten interpreters and the IS manager were interviewed. • Each interview lasted approximately forty-five minutes. • Interviews were conducted during work hours, under the provision (approved by the IS manager) that I would make up the interpreters' lost work. • Three main themes were discussed: (1) the parties for whom interpreting was done; (2) interpreters' participation in stressful situations; and (3) the role of the interpreter in an ICE.	• The tapes containing the interviews were fully transcribed into computer files. • The transcripts were then analyzed for emerging patterns, typicalities (differences and similarities were considered).

Interviews

Semi-structured, taped interviews were conducted with interpreters about their role. This yielded a set of recorded data. The process used in the collection, coding, and analysis of this data is presented in table 6.

Finding the time for an interview was problematic, because interpreters at CH simply have no free time. Interviewing them outside of their work hours would have required them to stay after hours or to give up their lunch break, which seemed like an unreasonable request on my part, so I presented an alternative solution to the manager. He would give them the time for my interview, and in exchange I would do the translation jobs that they would have been asked to do during that time. The manager agreed to this arrangement, with the provision that the interviews be scheduled through him, because he needed to know which codes the interpreters would key into their computers while they were in an interview. Through this system, I was able to interview the ten interpreters as well as the manager.

Each interview lasted approximately forty-five minutes. Three basic themes were discussed during the interviewing process: (1) the parties for whom interpretations were conducted; (2) interpreters' participation in stressful situations; and (3) the role of the interpreter in an ICE. I also interviewed the interpreters and the manager several times informally, taking handwritten notes during those sessions. The tapes containing the interviews were fully transcribed and then analyzed for emerging patterns.

Audio recordings of ICEs

In order to remain true to the purposes of this ethnographical study, it was important to obtain a sense of what each interpreter experienced during a regular workday and week. I spent a great amount of time at the site. By the time I started recording, I had already shadowed and monitored the ten Spanish interpreters for more than nine months. During the data collection, I tried to minimize my intrusion in the interaction and among the participants. Two or three times per week, I arrived at IS at 8:00 a.m. and spent the entire day with one interpreter. I connected a headset to their telephone, and the interpreters interacted with me as they did with other new interpreters in training. They were accustomed to having other people present during their interpreting sessions, or accompanying them on face-to-face assignments, because that is how new interpreters receive on-the-job training, but they had never been recorded. I asked many questions as I observed. While recording, my presence was made even more evident by the extra cable on the interpreters' desk: the one that connected my tape recorder to their phone.

Consent for recording and observing was requested at the outset of the interpreting session. During speakerphone interpretations, both HCP and patient were alerted to my presence and given the option to either give or withhold consent. On some occasions, consent was quickly granted. At other times, either HCP or patient asked questions as to the nature of the research, and an explanation was offered. Consent was only denied without asking about the nature of the research on four occasions.

At any given time during an ICE, the interpreter had the option of pressing the mute button in order to avoid the recording of a comment. Otherwise, the entire phone conversation was recorded. When interpreters received personal calls, I turned my recorder off and left the cubicle.

During face-to-face interpretations, I introduced myself to both patient and HCP, briefly explained the purpose of my study, and requested consent. I always tried to strategically place myself, as well as my tape recorder, in the least conspicuous place possible, where I could observe and record without intruding on the session. The interpreters usually briefed me on the nature of the interpreting on the way to the face-to-face interpreting sessions, since this usually involved walking a fair distance to different areas of the hospital. I utilized this time to ask questions and develop trust. Conversations were always friendly and sometimes personal. We became well acquainted through walks to and from interpreting assignments and while sitting in the cubicles waiting for calls.

During speakerphone interpreting, I tried not to overload interpreters with information-seeking questions between calls. So as not to occupy all of their downtime, I only pursued a question if they made a comment about the interpretation that they had just completed. For example, interpreters would often comment on the unnecessary and tiresome repetition of questions in the medical admitting clerks' protocols or on the part of the student doctors. At other times they would remark about the Spanish regional variety used by a patient and how it required clarification of certain terms. Other comments were centered around the kindness or rudeness of the parties involved or on the seriousness of the case, and the interpreter's personal reaction to it.

Since ICEs vary widely in a healthcare institution in terms of length and time of day, flexibility was essential in designing a plan for data collection. The data collection plan was often revised once or twice weekly. Sometimes, obtaining just one hour of recording required several days' work. There were constant unforeseen interruptions. On one occasion, I was shadowing an interpreter who was suddenly called away to attend a training session on the new fire alarm system. On another occasion, the interpreter I was shadowing was asked to cover for a dispatcher. Yet another was pulled away because of a rush-status translation assignment. Other times, interpreters needed to take breaks, or they worked irregular hours, since they also had to cover emergency situations. Collecting naturalistic data was not trivial, especially because it implied no special accommodation for timing on the part of the interpreters. I often switched back and forth between two interpreters in the same day.

A total of five ninety-minute tapes of naturalistic data were collected from each of the ten interpreters while at work. The fifty tapes yielded 392 ICEs. A summary of the procedure used for collection, coding, and analysis of data is presented in table 7.

Table 7 *Audio recordings of interpreted communicative events*

Collection	Coding and analysis
• A tape recorder and an extra headset were connected to the interpreter's telephone during the interpreting session. • Consent for recording and observing was requested at the outset of the session. During speakerphone sessions, both HCP and patient were alerted to my presence in the interaction and were given the option to give or withhold consent. (During the 22 months of data collection, consent was denied only on four occasions.) During face-to-face interpreting sessions, I requested consent. The tape recorder was always placed in the least conspicuous location possible. • Five 90-minute tapes were collected from each of the ten interpreters, yielding 392 ICEs.	• Five tapes were produced for each of the ten interpreters; they were labeled with tape number, interpreter's name, and date. • A 153-page computerized index was made from the tapes, containing entries for each ICE. Each entry contained detailed information about the ICE (duration; gender and position of all participants). In paragraph format of approximately fifteen to twenty-two lines, each entry contained a summary of the interaction, including a transcript of certain excerpts with exact tape location. Several copies were made of the index. • One copy was used for unit analysis. There were 392 ICEs. Annotations (codes) were penciled in beside each unit to allow for correction, based on category fluctuation or solidification. These codes constituted the basis of subsequent emerging categories and patterns (LeCompte and Schensul 1999). The pattern of the nature of the ICE generated two objective categories which required no corroboration: face-to-face and speakerphone. • Another copy was used to study the intention of the interaction. Six categories of patterns emerged: make an appointment; place a phone call; deliver news/result; visit/check; educational session; and other/miscellaneous. Two of the informants were then interviewed about the kinds of calls they receive. They were asked to comment about the six categories. Their feedback confirmed that the initial etic perspective coincided with that of the informants, converting it into an emic perspective (LeCompte and Schensul 1999:221). It also served as corroboration for these six categories. • A third copy of the index was used to explore the interpreter's intervention or lack thereof during the ICEs, and the reason behind those behaviors. These behaviors were first coded in the margin, stating characteristics of the interpersonal role that transpired from the interaction across interpreters and across nature, and the intention of the ICEs analyzed. Some examples are: solidarity and power (Tannen 1984); editing by omitting or adding (Davidson 1998); interpreter as principal interlocutor (Roy 2000); and interpreter as facilitating understanding (Davidson 1998). Two informants were then interviewed and asked to comment on the emerging patterns. Their feedback corroborated the idea of visibility.

Call 2
Side A 087 – 424 and Side B 000-043
SD student female/ P female
SD consents 091. I positions and introduces self and requests consent 094. HI: "yes doctor, we are ready" reason for coming 097 and general questions 107. HI uses 1st person pronoun when answering for Mom 111 and then erratically "they used to live in Mexico..." 119. D: Was it because she did not like the food in Mexico? HI: "¿no cree usted que era un poco ridículo, no le gustaban las cosas en México, la comida?"123 P: "¿Mande? No sé" HI: "She doesn't know." Mom explains other illness. 133. HI explores last time she had pain 137. Mom constantly compares how child was worse when they lived in Mexico 148. Mom blames water quality 152. HI explores frequency of complaints due to pain HI: "como digamos en una semana, ¿cuántas veces se queja?" 169. Mom answers with stories. 175. Mom does not know how much the girl weighed before they came to the US. 185 D: "What sorts of things does she eat?" HI: ¿Qué es lo que la niña come, señora, más o menos denos un ejemplo?" 192 HI: "¿Qué más señora?" 195 HI elicits without waiting for D to ask –Rashes explored 238. Fever 245. HI: "¿le tomaron rayos X del torax, señora?" P: "sí" HI: "Y ¿qué le dijeron?" 261 <I explores without waiting to be told. >. Hepatitis explored. Mom does not know type 267 and does not remember medication intake 290. HI paraphrases other medical problems 310 into "¿problema de salud como asma o ataques epilépticos o problemas de corazón, otra cosa?" P: "como somos de ciudad Juarez, allí hace mucho frío" HI: "they use to live in the north part of Mexico" 324 <I inserts comment of location due to own knowledge>. D: "Normal delivery? Was she breast fed?" <All those D questions get explored as "¿le dio usted pecho o le dio botella? ¿Nació normal, de 9 meses, alguna complicación con el parto, cesárea o parto normal?" I constantly explores and explains options. 345. Other symptoms explored. D: Do her stools float or do they sink? HI: "Señora, cuando la niña va al baño, ¿usted le ve el excremento o ella nada más va solita, se limpia y eso es todo?" <HI decided to first elicit if Mom sees stool or not and then explores stool> 394. Mom asks child "no se acuerda m'hija si se queda arriba o se va pa'bajo" 400. Neither Mom nor child remember. Anything else 418. ICE interrupted to turn tape at 422 while HI explores other people living at home 003. Side B Cont. Medical problems in the family 006. Urination problems 008. P: "a veces trae bien irritada su colita 010" < HI makes comment about the term colita to me and presses mute button: "Ni que fuera un animal!!" SES> HI does not convey this redness in the colita. Fluid intake 028. D will examine child 041. Bye thanks 043 <HI does not say bye to Mom > 043 - Duration 30:00

Figure 6   Example of an index entry of an ICE

I used the computerized index as a quick reference guide to the transcripts. The language in the index reflects what each of the interlocutors used. Figure 6 shows an entry of an ICE between a female patient (P) and a female student doctor (SD). The interpreter (I) is Mariana. This entry demonstrates the level of detail that goes into a thirty-minute interaction. The numbers represent the exact locations in the tape. These entries were used for unit analysis and for the identification of categories and subcategories of the ICEs.

Several copies were made of the index. One of these copies was used for unit analysis. The pattern of the nature of the ICE generated two categories: face-to-face and over-the-speakerphone. Another copy was used to study the intention of the interaction. Six categories emerged from patterns of the intention of the interaction of the ICE: (1) schedule an appointment; (2) place a phone call; (3) deliver news or results; (4) provide health education; (5) plan a visit or checkup; and (6) other.

A third copy of the index entries was used to explore the last pattern that emerged in terms of the interpreter's intervention or lack thereof during ICEs, and the reason behind those behaviors. These interventions or behaviors were first coded on the margin, stating characteristics of the interpersonal role that transpired from the interaction across interpreters and across the nature and the intention of the ICEs analyzed. I called this pattern visibility of the interpreter. Visibility, as we have seen, means that the interpreter's role extends beyond the role of language switcher. The interpreter does not simply decode and encode the parties' messages cross-linguistically to bridge a communication gap (as generally described in the literature or prescribed by the professional associations). Triggered by the interplay of social factors, a visible interpreter expands beyond the transparent language boom box to the opaque co-participant and exercises agency within the interaction. Agency manifests itself when interpreters do one or more of the following: (1) introduce or position the self as a party to the ICE, becoming co-participants (Roy 2000; Wadensjö 1998) and co-constructors (Davidson 1998); (2) set communication rules and control the traffic of information (Roy 2000); (3) paraphrase or explain terms or concepts (Davidson 1998); (4) slide the message up and down the register scale (Interview with Mariana: see chapter 7); (5) filter information (Davidson 1998); (6) align with one of the parties (Wadensjö 1998); and (7) replace one of the parties to the ICE (Roy 2000).

In order to assure that the categories were stable, I looked at the frequency and the stability of visibility across interpreters. Of the 392 ICEs, 5 percent were invisible[2] and 95 percent were visible. Out of the ten interpreters observed, behaviors of visibility were identified in all of them. For four of the interpreters, all ICEs were visible (100 percent). For the six interpreters in whom invisibility was found, it ranged from a minimum of 4 percent to a maximum of 12 percent. Table 8 illustrates the categories of data that emerged when the entire corpus was analyzed. Out of 392 events analyzed, 378 (96.4 percent) showed some degree of interpreter's visibility while only 14 (3.6 percent) resulted in interpreter's invisibility. The interpreters who produced invisible renditions were Rogelio (5 of 45, or 11.1 percent), Consuelo (4 of 54, or 7.4 percent), Marcos (2 of 32, or 6.2 percent) and Julio, Mauro, and Mariana (1 of 25, 46 and 39, or 4 percent, 2.1 percent and 2.6 percent respectively).

---

[2] This percentage occurred in the shortest ICEs (under three minutes). It is not discussed further since, in the tradition of ethnography of communication, my research addresses typicality. The two extremes of very invisible and very visible fall out of the continuum of degrees of visibility present at CH.

Table 8 *Inventory of interpreted communicative events*

Interpreter	# of ICEs	Visible	Invisible	Face-to-face	Phone	Make appointment	Place phone call	News/ results	Educational	Visit/ check	Other
Mariana	39	38	1	2	37	11	0	0	1	25	2
Julio	25	24	1	2	23	5	0	1	0	18	1
Vicente	24	24	0	1	23	11	0	0	1	12	0
Rogelio	45	40	5	1	44	23	1	0	0	18	3
Consuelo	54	50	4	2	52	18	0	0	0	32	4
Mauro	46	45	1	0	46	8	0	0	0	35	3
Marcos	32	30	2	0	32	9	1	2	5	13	2
Joaquín	50	50	0	0	50	17	2	1	0	27	3
Annette	37	37	0	2	35	6	6	0	2	22	1
Elda	40	40	0	1	39	12	0	0	0	28	0
TOTAL	392	378	14	11	381	120	10	4	9	230	19

The analysis of the visibility and invisibility identified for each interpreter was carried out on two separate occasions using unmarked index copies, in order to ensure consistency in the identification procedure. Figure 7 illustrates an excerpt from an entry where visibility is identified. The segments where visibility is identified are marked between < > brackets, and the emerging subcategories of intention of the interaction (described above) are in bold type. In the paper copy used, colored Post-it markers were used for the different subcategories. In this example, P stands for patient, N is for nurse, and HI for interpreter. The numbers correspond to the locations on the tape. In this entry, examples of subcategories of visibility are present. The same numbers of tape locations show the instances of visibility that had been marked:

004 HI is co-participant: evidenced by taking turn to introduce self.
013–019 HI is co-participant: evidenced by taking turn to explore.
020 HI summarizes P's information; HI filters by exercising power.
029 HI paraphrases to help P understand the term chronic illness; solidarity.
047–049 HI corners P; HI gets answer by exercising power.
051 HI summarizes for N and expresses frustration at P's behavior; power.
054 HI controls traffic and does not let P interrupt; power.
059–061 HI edits what P says and summarizes story; power.
061–067 HI explores; own initiative; power/solidarity.
068 HI interrupts P's story and relays information to N; power.
069–071 HI gets addressed by N and HI talks about P with N; power, alignment.
078 HI is asked to explain a procedure for obtaining a primary care physician, but is not given the words. HI takes initiative; resorts to his/her own knowledge.

Bold terms are examples of subcategories identified. Subcategories were considered temporary until they stabilized. The entire corpus of data was subjected to this procedure.

Categories and subcategories emerging from ICEs

As mentioned earlier, the observation and recording of ten interpreters yielded 392 ICEs. The maximum number of ICEs done by one interpreter was fifty-four and the minimum was twenty-four, with an average of thirty-nine.

Nature of the ICE

Face-to-face   The interpreter is physically present at the scene where the ICE takes place. Of 392 ICEs observed, 3 percent were face-to-face.

Descriptors	Content summary
Tape 09 000-087 Mariana 2/1/99 Nurse female Patient male Duration: 12:00 minutes	N consents 003. P info 004. HI positions and introduces self <**active participant**>and requests consent 009. P starts: "tengo muchas complicaciones, ¿me entiende?" HI: "¿qué tipo de complicaciones tiene?" 013 < **explores own initiative**> P explains is incontinent. P: "hace mucho" HI: OK, "¿cuánto es mucho para usted?" < HI **continues to explore, takes lead**> 016. HI **continues to explore previous medical condition** 019. N: "Mariana, I don't know if he is a new patient or what. I have to get that first" 020. N was left out. HI **summarizes for N** while P continues to tell story. N needs info 022 (telephone, birthday) <**interesting, N is on one track and P on another**> HI paraphrases chronic illness 029 < **paraphrasing-convergence**>. N is blunt in tone "reason he is calling today?", seems she wants to be in control while P is upset because he is constantly interrupted while telling story 040. Reason for call gets answered in 047. P is upset with hospital not answering or paying any attention to his problem 049. HI **corners** him to get an answer she can relay <HI caught **in between controlling forces??? Agency??**> "OK, pero ¿cuál es el problema por el que quieren que lo vean hoy?" P: "TODO (upsetting tone)" 049 HI: "Oh my god! Well...we don't have really hmmm a reason ... Why he wants to be seen..." 051 <HI: **explains** what is going on, **filters** P's reaction P is upset and expects HI to sympathize with him. N is upset and expects HI to comply with line of questions!!! **HI seems to align with more powerful party!!!** > "he says all these problems ... so let me tell you what he said" and HI **summarizes** for N 054. P interrupts "bueno" 054 and I replies "un momentito señor" <visibility, **traffic control**> 054. N double checks and HI answers <without checking back with P: **participant**> 059. HI checks one thing only with P and he answers back with another story inserting more stuff and **gets controlled by HI** 061. HI **explores** the "getting mad part" 066 HI: "¿Cuándo fue la última vez que vino a ver al doctor y se fue porque no quería esperar más tiempo?" 066 P: "No, no... no es que no quise esperar más tiempo. Fui y me tuvieron como cinco horas ahí" HI: "(overlaps) Oh... fue a la emergencia" 067. P: "Sí, y luego de la emergencia no me dieron más que dos pastillas y me echaron pa' fuera, no fue..." 068 HI **interrupts** and relays info to N <**power/lack of solidarity**>. N: "Mariana, I am not going to make him an appointment.." HI: (overlaps) "I know" N: (overlaps) "these are not urgent cares. Urgent care will kill me" 071 <interesting **chain of pressure. Alignment with hospital**> N: **could you explain to him....** <HI **explains procedure to P**, needs to have a PCP> 078. P complains 079, he had already done this. 081. P is transferred to get an appointment. "Thanks, no cuelgue, bye" 087

Figure 7   Example of visibility in an index entry

Speakerphone   The interpreter is physically removed from the scene where the ICE takes place. The interpreter is in a remote office, performing the interpretation over the telephone. Of 392 ICEs, observed 97 percent were conducted over the speakerphone.

Intention of the ICE

According to their intention, ICEs were classified as follows:

Schedule an appointment   When a patient calls to make an appointment, the call is first handled by a medical admitting clerk who verifies the patient's background information, asks questions about the reason for the appointment, and routes the call accordingly. Then, the patient and interpreter in tandem are transferred to a nurse, a counselor, an educator, or a physician for a thorough protocol according to the patient's needs (assessed by the medical admitting clerk). After this is done, the HCP can schedule an appointment on the basis of need and availability.

Place a phone call   This occurs when one of either a patient or an HCP needs to call the other. Calls are usually related to appointment scheduling (reminders, cancellations, or re-scheduling).

Deliver news or results   This occurs when an HCP reports a test result to a patient, or reports on a decision made by a group of experts regarding the patient's case. This also occurs when a patient calls CH to solicit the results of a test.

Provide health education   This refers to instances where a patient comes to the hospital for an educational session. For example, diabetic patients attend classes on diet and on proper use of the glucometer (an instrument used by the patient at home to monitor blood glucose levels). Pregnant women attend prenatal sessions; courses are offered for wheelchair-bound patients with spinal cord injuries on how to bathe themselves and how to get around the house in their wheelchair.

Plan a visit or check-up   Patients can see an HCP either for a check-up or for a specific procedure. For example, adult patients come in for Pap smears or CT scans. Children are brought in for vaccines. Cancer patients are monitored for signs of recurrent disease.

Other   This category encompasses various reasons for seeking interpreting services. Patients who call to enquire about a bill received from the hospital and are accidentally transferred to IS (because they speak Spanish) fall within this category. Another situation that occurs commonly is when Spanish-speaking family members call the hospital in attempts to locate a relative who is hospitalized.

Visibility of the interpreter

ICEs were classified according to where they fell within the visibility–invisibility continuum discussed above. Extreme cases were observed on only two occasions and are pointed out in the discussion as exemptions that confirm the average degree of visibility of interpreters.

In this chapter, we have discussed the procedure to collect, code, and analyze the data obtained at CH. At the beginning of chapter 4, Vygotsky reminded us that it is only in movement that a body shows what it is. Both chapters 4 and 5 have set the stage and the form in which the movement takes place. In the next two chapters, I hold that movement still as we take a detailed look at the role of the interpreter at CH.

6   Finding visibility

> I would argue that translation for the philologist – one who would guide us
> across the terra incognita between distant languages – is not the final goal, but
> only a first step, in understanding a distant text; necessary because it opens
> up for us the exuberances and deficiencies of our own interpretations and so
> helps us see what kinds of self-correction must be made.
>
> <div align="right">A. L. Becker <i>Beyond Translation</i> (1995:186)</div>

The nature of the ICE at California Hope

The ICEs at CH cover a range of activities and, as we have seen, occur either
over the speakerphone or face-to-face. Patients or HCPs need interpreters to
assist them in performing various activities and carrying out communicative
functions. Examples of activities include: making or canceling an appointment;
delivering news or results; conducting a verbal examination (speech pathology);
conducting a physical examination (physician); conducting a procedure (e.g. CT
scan); and calling to remind about an appointment. In these activities, any of the
following communicative functions can occur: complain, request, reprimand;
explain, express support, justify, advise; ask and answer questions, express
solidarity; instruct; inform; and remind. The length of the ICE also varies significantly, according to the nature of the event (which varies from two minutes
to over two hours). For example, an appointment cancellation or a reminder
call may take under three minutes. These ICEs are generally conducted over
the telephone. A check-up visit may take fifteen minutes, with the interpreter
present or at a remote location (over the speakerphone). A CT scan, where all
three parties are face-to-face, can take two hours.

It is also evident that ICEs at CH vary significantly from ICEs in other settings, such as a court of law or a business conference. This variation among
settings may lie in the expectations of the role of the interpreter and the interactions between the participants. In a court of law, the role of the interpreter
is highly regulated (Berk-Seligson 1990). The expectations for such a role are
very clear: the interpreter must interpret verbatim and refrain from having any
direct conversation with the defendant. If the interpreter, for example, needs

to clarify a term, he/she must ask permission from the court before doing so (NAJIT 2003).

In a conference setting, such as a business or political meeting, the interaction between the interpreters and the speakers is not as abundant as in a medical or court setting. The interpreter is expected to follow one speaker at a time, and the interaction between the parties is usually limited to the question-and-answer period (Roy 2000; Wadensjö 1998). The interaction between interpreter and parties is also usually limited to the question-and-answer period. Thus, the role that the interpreter plays at CH (or any other medical or community setting) is considerably different from these other settings. It is different from the role of the court interpreter, because the latter is more tightly regulated and is constrained by laws and rules to speak and behave in a certain way. It is different from the role of the conference interpreter since, when working from a booth, he/she is physically limited to interact (or rather not to interact) with the other parties in a certain way. Also, when working from a booth, the channels of communication impose a monologic mode upon the conference interpreter (Wadensjö 1998). These differences point to a greater freedom in the co-construction of the role on the part of the medical interpreter.

Given the dialogic nature of a medical interview and how it differs from a monologic event, such as a speech during a conference or a judge's ruling, one might argue that the visibility of the interpreter could be related only to situations of spontaneous talk and not to planned talk (Levy 1999). It could also be argued that visibility depends on the setting being private instead of public. The protocols utilized during the medical encounter appear to hybridize planned and spontaneous talk. They usually begin with an exploratory phase in which there is room for spontaneous talk and discovery, and then they move into a tighter line of questioning focused on the patient's chief complaint. Since interpreters were found to be invisible in a small percentage of cases (4 percent) in the medical interactions observed at CH (where there were instances of planned and spontaneous talk in the same interaction), I suggest that the visibility of the interpreter may have more to do with the nature of the setting than with the type of talk. As discussed in chapter 3, the presence of an audience has a significant impact on discourse (Irvine 1992). Unlike court and conference interpreting that are public in nature, medical interpreting generally occurs in a private setting (exceptions being conferences with patients, family members, insurance companies, hospital administrators, or members of the healthcare team) where no audience is present. This setting, however, may afford the interpreter more instances to be visible.

The structure of the ICE at California Hope

Like any other communicative event, an ICE is characterized by having an opening, a body, and a closing. Like any monolingual medical consultation, an ICE can also be divided into the six phases that Byrne and Long (1976) identify in their study of the verbal behaviors of 2,000 medical consultations. These phases include: (1) relating to the patient; (2) discovering the reason for attendance; (3) conducting a verbal or physical examination or both; (4) considering the patient's condition; (5) detailing treatment or further investigation; and (6) terminating. Contrary to a monolingual medical consultation, an ICE consists of three participants; the presence of an interpreter in the ICE impacts on those six phases.

Interpreter visibility: an overview

As stated in chapter 1, for an interpreter to be visible in the interaction, it means that the interpreter's role goes beyond that of a language switcher. The job of the interpreter involves more than just providing an accurate cross-linguistic decoding and encoding of the parties' messages (as prescribed by the professional associations). Previous research has established that interpreters are in fact co-participants in terms of the linguistic manipulations and their moves during talk. This active role was explored by Berk-Seligson (1990) in her ethnography of a courtroom. By manipulating the use of polite forms (for example, using a more polite or less polite way of addressing one of the parties; restating an utterance in different forms by adding or omitting jargonistic remarks; or switching from formal to informal register), interpreters in the bilingual courtroom can alter their visibility status. Studies of immigration hearings at a police station (Wadensjö 1995), of medical encounters between Swedish and Russian speakers (Wadensjö 1992), and between English and ASL speakers (Metzger 1999), as well as community encounters such as professor–student conferences (Roy 2000), also demonstrate evidence of the visible role of interpreters through their moves during talk. Through analysis of discourse (focusing on how interpreters get addressed in talk, address others, coordinate talk, and manage communication), these researchers have established that the interpreter is a co-participant who takes an active role in conversational interpreted events (Roy 2000:44–6) or dialogic interpreting (Wadensjö 1998). The analytical tool of looking at transcriptions of interpreted recorded talk, used by Wadensjö, Roy, and Metzger, clearly points out the interpreter's participation in the interaction. In establishing the interpreter as a co-conversationalist, these researchers have helped the field to move away from the conceptualization of the interpreter as a conduit. Now that the participation of the interpreter is established, the question that follows is: what triggers that participation?

Looking at the interpreter's participation in the interaction, Wadensjö studied interpreter renditions as translation of text and as coordination of talk. To explore the translation of text, she developed a taxonomy (1998:106–8) of interpreters' utterances to account for the renditions of the originals (sources) they interpret. Her taxonomy is mostly based on a comparison of the propositional context present in the original utterance and the rendition rather than on the different types of equivalences (lexical, grammatical, and pragmatic) (1998: 42). She also looked at the interpreter's role in coordinating talk and how that coordination can be implicit (interpreter's talk) or explicit (request for clarification or requests to observe turn-taking order) (1998:107–8). This taxonomy and classification of coordination are essential in order for us to see the interpreter's participation. In this study, I go a step beyond the work done by other researchers, and explore what triggers interpreters' participation. Since interpreters are social beings who participate in an interaction that does not occur in a social vacuum, I propose a model of a visible interpreter (see figure 3) whose participation is on the one hand triggered by the interplay of social factors and, on the other hand, constrained by the norms of the institution and the society in which the interaction occurs. To consider this model and the social factors that trigger the interpreter's participation I suggest the interplay of the three lenses introduced in chapter 3. In the next sections, I present segments of talk and explore the social factors that trigger interpreters' interventions. This work should be construed as an expansion of the work of researchers such as Metzger, Roy, and Wadensjö, since it addresses questions that go beyond the findings of interpreters as co-participants. It addresses the question of the social factors that trigger interpreters' increasing ownership of text. By creating their own renditions, interpreters become visible.

A visible interpreter is one who exercises agency within the interaction, in order to bridge a communication gap. This agency manifests itself through text ownership. The fact that interpreters perceive the need to create text (i.e. produce utterances not originally produced by the interlocutors for reasons other than translating or clarifying, as suggested by Wadensjö in 1998) is a manifestation of visibility. According to their amount of involvement in creating text ownership, interpreters can be either more or less visible. Thus, an ICE might have only original messages transmitted by the two parties, a combination of original messages and interpreter-owned messages, or interpreter-owned messages only. It could be said, then, that all ICEs lie along a continuum that stretches between these two points of high and low visibility on the part of the interpreters.

Manifestations of visibility in ICEs at California Hope

In all of the ICEs at CH, visibility seems to be a fluid concept with a number of variable dimensions. Visibility varies according to the location of the ICE. It occurs in the opening and closing, as well as in the body of the ICE (i.e. the different phases of the medical interview). Visibility that occurs during the openings and closings is highly ritualized (Goffman 1981). If the HCP does not introduce the interpreter during openings, the interpreter introduces and positions him/herself. Any co-participant to an interaction would do as much, in order to claim status.

During closings, the interpreter has already established a relationship, which needs to be closed. This is expected of any co-participant in any relationship. The ICEs at CH abide by conversational rituals, similar to those of monolingual communicative events. Because of the highly ritualized nature of openings and closings, I do not consider them to be part of the visibility continuum (shown in figure 8). They will be discussed separately.

Visibility varies in terms of intensity. According to the level of the interpreter's participation (ownership in text) in the co-construction of the event, ICEs at CH illustrate instances of the entire spectrum of visibility. Toward the low end of the visibility spectrum (minor visibility), we see instances in which there is occasional involvement of the interpreter as co-owner of the text. At the high end of the visibility continuum (major visibility) lie situations in which the interpreter is the owner of the text. In this analysis of interpreters' perceptions of their role, the intensity of visibility is determined by text ownership and not by linguistic effectuations of strategies, such as variation in the use of pronouns.

Becoming visible: linguistic and communicative strategies

The linguistic and communicative strategies used by interpreters to render interpreter-owned messages are varied. In some cases, interpreters are slightly involved in the production of text by the use of a single pronoun (they include themselves in an interaction); in other cases, interpreters produce messages that add significantly to those produced by the original interlocutors, thus navigating major and minor degrees of visibility. For example, if a doctor uses a technical term, such as clear liquid diet, the interpreter takes ownership by expanding, explaining, or changing the register for the patient, in order to ensure that the patient understands. Clear liquids then become water, broth, and apple juice.

Figure 8 illustrates several strategies used by interpreters to convey interpreter-owned messages. Some of these strategies are highly consequential, and others are less so. When looking at this continuum, one must bear in mind that the order in which the categories (strategies) are presented is unstable and the borderlines are fluid (i.e. each category could float under a different analytical approach). In the present study of visibility, I view the interpreter's strategies to take over ownership of text as being triggered by social factors, such as the patient's ethnicity, level of education, and socio-economic status, among others. I conjecture that the interpreter uses the strategies necessary to fulfill the communicative goals within the constraints that they face (chapter 3), either by the norms of the institution or the society where the encounter takes place or the circumstances surrounding it (e.g. with or without an audience).

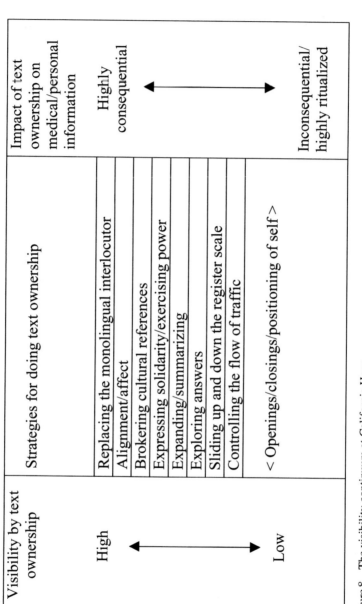

Figure 8   The visibility continuum at California Hope

At CH, interpreters take different steps to achieve their communicative goals, depending upon the social reality of all the participants involved in the encounter and the constraints that the institution imposes upon them.

In the next two sections, we will examine the continuum of visibility in more detail. We begin by looking at examples[1] of minor visibility that cooccur during openings and closings which correspond to, respectively, phases 1 (relating to patient) and 6 (terminating) of the medical interview.

Minor visibility: occasional involvement of interpreter as co-owner of text

Typical openings of an ICE

In relating to the patient, both HCP and interpreter act independently and relate to the patient separately. In other words, all ICEs at CH begin with either the patient or the HCP (whoever initiates the interaction) briefing the interpreter on the nature of the event for which they need help. If, for example, the HCP initiates the call for an interpreter, it is customary for the HCP to provide the interpreter with the name of the patient and the medical record number before briefing the interpreter about the case. If the patient initiates the call, the interpreter requests this information from the patient, together with the name of the HCP or service the patient is trying to reach. The interpreter then attempts to assess the patient's needs.

During an ICE at CH, the HCP and the patient reveal their identities, and the interpreter also introduces and positions him/herself. In some cases, interpreters merely state their name. Sometimes they add a comment about how they are ready to help the parties communicate, as can be seen in segments 1 and 2. At other times, interpreters state the fact that they work for CH, thus positioning themselves within the institution. Segment 3 is an example of this variation.

In the first example (segment 1), Joaquín,[2] who is interpreting over the speakerphone, facilitates the communication between a middle-aged Spanish-speaking female patient and an English-speaking female nurse who are face-to-face in an office. The nurse is asking questions in order to gather information about the patient. The ICE is fifteen minutes long. The interaction begins when

---

[1] The level of detail included in the transcriptions of the speech of HCPs, patients, and interpreters is adequate for the type of analysis performed. Overlaps are signaled, and the English translations of Spanish utterances are included. The following conventions are adopted:
  – *Italics*: text in Spanish
  – (parentheses): English glosses of Spanish utterances
  – [brackets]: overlapping utterances (used to mark the point at which an utterance in progress is joined by another interrupting utterance)
  – ▶ is used to call attention to the turn discussed

[2] For demographic information on CH interpreters, refer to table 2 in chapter 4.

the nurse (N) tells Joaquín (HI) the patient's name (P), before the patient comes into the conversation. Joaquín repeats the name (turn 1), and as the patient enters the conversation, Joaquín greets her and introduces himself.

Segment 1: Joaquín (Tape 0: 001–007)

1	HI	¿María Gómez?
2	N	Gómez. Thank you. Here she is.
3 ▶	HI	*Señora. Buenos días.*
		(Ma'am, good morning.)
4	P	*Sí. Buenos días.*
		(Yes. Good morning.)
5 ▶	HI	*Soy un intérprete, me llamo Joaquín y le voy a ayudar a platicar con la enfermera.*
		(I am an interpreter. My name is Joaquín, and I am going to help you talk with the nurse.)
6	P	*Okay.*

Joaquín describes to the patient his role as both an interpreter and a helper (turn 5). This turn is not given to him; he chooses to position himself as a helper. He does not just state that he is going to interpret between María Gómez and the nurse. Instead, he positions himself as an active participant in this interaction. In subsequent informal interviews with Joaquín, he refers to patients as concerned individuals who bring their sufferings and fears to the medical appointment. He mentions repeatedly the fact that his role is to make sure that their fears are addressed. The impression he forms from these patients (Brewer 1988 in chapter 3) triggers a sense of solidarity in Joaquín, and he believes he addresses the patients' fears by expressing this solidarity.

In segment 2 Elda (HI) is brokering communication between a male English-speaking doctor (D) and a male Spanish-speaking patient (P). What precedes segment 2 is the interaction between the doctor and Elda. When the doctor tells Elda the patient's name, she recognizes the name from having worked with him in the past. The patient, Julio, is coming to the urology clinic, and we join them when Elda greets Julio.

Segment 2: Elda (Tape 23: 234–238)

1	HI	*Julio, buenas tardes.*
		(Julio, good afternoon.)
2	P	*Buenas tardes.*
		(Good afternoon.)
3 ▶	HI	*¿Cómo ha estado? Habla Elda, yo sé que ya me reconoció.*
		(How have you been? This is Elda. I know that you recognized me.)
4	P	*Ajá.*
		(Aha.)
5 ▶	HI	*Ese ajá quiere decir sí, verdad? . . . Ya lo conozco.* Okay doctor.
		(That aha means yes, right? . . . I know you.)

Finding visibility 81

The way in which Elda addresses the patient on a first-name basis (turn 1) leads us to believe that this is not her first encounter with Julio. This becomes evident at turn 3 when Elda asks the patient how he has been, and she states that she is aware that Julio has already recognized her voice. The first three exchanges between Elda and Julio are not shared with the doctor. The only information that Elda relays to the doctor is that they are ready to start the interview (turn 5). These exchanges between interpreter and patient are typical of interactions between interpreters and patients who have worked together in the past. They have already established a relationship which they honor by greeting each other directly. Following this observation, I asked Elda about Julio, and how long she has known him. She said that she remembers him well, and then she spoke about his health issues and the many times she has interpreted for him. She also mentioned that she recognized his voice, how gentle and respectful he had always been, and his sense of humor. She always enjoyed helping him. From these remarks we can see how Elda relates to the patient, how she orients toward him (Festinger 1954 in chapter 3), and how she builds upon a relationship already established, even when the interaction occurs over the speakerphone.

Segment 3 comes from a six-minute ICE in which a male English-speaking doctor (D) and a female Spanish-speaking patient (P) are face-to-face in the urgent care clinic when Mariana (HI) enters the setting from the speakerphone. She first listens to the doctor's briefing on the patient and thanks him for that. We come in when she is about to introduce herself to the patient.

Segment 3: Mariana (Tape 11: 040–047)

1 ▶ HI Thank you, doctor. Let me introduce myself to the patient.
Señora María Cabrera, buenos días.
(Mrs. María Cabrera, good morning.)

2 P *Buenos días.*
(Good morning.)

3 ▶ HI *Mire señora, yo soy una intérprete de este hospital y le voy a ayudar para que pueda comunicarse con el doctor Pang.*
(I am an interpreter in this hospital and I am going to help you so that you can communicate with Dr. Pang.)

4 P *Sí.*
(Yes.)

5 HI We are ready doctor.

Mariana, like Joaquín, positions herself as a helper. Unlike Joaquín however, Mariana states that she is a helper, affiliated with the institution. In subsequent conversations with Mariana, she told me that she felt a part of the healthcare team. She, like all other interpreters, works with providers for the wellbeing of the patient. This belief may explain why Mariana always identifies herself as a member of the institution for which she works.

What is interesting about these three opening segments is that when the interpreters introduce themselves to the patients, the lines are never given to them by HCPs. How interpreters decide to talk, and what they want to say are under their own control. Sometimes what they say is triggered by the interplay of patient's and interpreter's ethnicity, sense of solidarity, or affect, all of which are social factors. Other times, we see the impact of the institution for whom interpreters work (when they identify with it) or how interpreters remain faithful to the way in which conversations are opened in their own culture, regardless of how the physician opens it. They claim their position as co-interlocutors, and in doing so, they obtain ownership of the lines they use.

Typical closings of an ICE

When the ICE is coming to a close, the parties give signals or cues to each other. Each person has his/her own way of ending the conversation; interpreters have their way too. As we saw during the openings, the interpreter develops ownership of a greeting line. The same occurs in the closings. Additionally, interpreters bring the relationship they have developed with each of the mono-lingual interlocutors to a closing. Segments 4, 5, and 6 illustrate this.

Segment 4 comes from an ICE between a Mexican Spanish-speaking female patient (P) and an English-speaker male doctor (D), brokered by Marcos (HI). The visit at the psychiatric ward is about to conclude. The doctor finishes examining the patient, and in closing he asks if there are any other questions. To that prompt, the patient responds that she wants to know the results of her previous lab tests. The doctor explains that her test results are normal, except that they indicate that she is anemic and will need another blood test. He also says that he will only call her if there is a problem. Otherwise he will see her at the next appointment. Marcos relays this information to the patient. After this, the doctor says goodbye (turn 1).

		Segment 4: Marcos (Tape 39: 171–173)
1	D ▶	Yeah! Bye bye. Thank you.
2	HI ▶	You are welcome doctor . . . *Hasta luego señora y ¡buena suerte!* (Goodbye Ma'am and good luck.)
3	P ▶	*¡Gracias!* (Thank you.)
4	HI ▶	Bye bye.
5	D ▶	Bye bye.

Marcos closes his interaction with the doctor (turn 2), and then does the same with the patient as he wishes her good luck. The patient (turn 3), like the doctor (turn 1), also thanks Marcos for his help. This segment illustrates typical behaviors of interpreters at the closing of ICEs. Interpreters at CH almost always expand on the lines to say goodbye (turn 2). While HCPs only close the ICE by saying thank you or goodbye, interpreters deliver expanded renditions (Wadensjö 1998) by always expressing solidarity to patients by wishing them: *que tenga un buen día*; *que le vaya bien*; *que se mejore*; or *mucha suerte* (hope you have a good day; hope everything is fine; hope you get better; good luck to you). In doing this, interpreters follow the rules of politeness of the patient, and they close the ICE accordingly. Doctors do not give those lines to interpreters. The interpreters themselves create them. In my discussions with Marcos, he repeatedly mentions the need to be polite with patients who might feel offended if they are not greeted in the norms of their culture. Marcos' awareness of this may explain his expression of solidarity at turn 2. Marcos forms an impression of the patient and the doctor during this ICE. According to theories on interpersonal relations, Marcos develops his system of categories (Brewer 1988 in chapter 3) for both the patient and the doctor and uses this system to bridge the cultural gap at the close of the encounter. He realizes that the doctor has finished and has not closed properly, and he also realizes that the patient expects a closing.

Segment 5 presents the closing of an ICE between a female English-speaking medical admitting clerk (M) and a Spanish-speaking patient (P). The ICE is interpreted by Consuelo (HI). The patient is calling CH, because her child has a problem. She already has an appointment for later in the month (the 26th) but wants to see if there is an earlier opening. Unfortunately, no appointments are available, so the clerk suggests that the patient keep her appointment. When we join the ICE, the clerk is explaining this to Consuelo and signaling the end of the exchange.

Segment 5: Consuelo (Tape 45: 234–296)

1	M	She should be keeping that appointment for the 26 . . . um . . . and then . . . you know . . . if she has any questions or problems before then she can hmm . . . give us a call.
2	HI	Okay.
3	M	Okay . . . but . . . as far as . . . you know . . . moving her up sooner. . . . He has no opening before then?
4	HI ▶	*Usted va a tener que mantener esa cita. No vaya a perder su cita del día veintiseis.* (You have to keep your appointment. You should not miss your appointment on the 26th.)
5	P	*Muy bien.* (Fine.)
6	HI ▶	*Okay . . . ahora bien . . . si de aquí para el veintiseis surge algún problema . . . algo . . . entonces nos llama . . . nos llama aquí para hacerlo saber . . . Okay?* (Okay . . . but . . . if between now and the 26th there is any problem . . . anything . . . then you call us . . . you call us to let us know . . . Okay?)

7	P		*Claro que sí.*
			(Of course.)
8	HI	▶	*¿Okay? Y se lo hacemos saber al doctor Jacob . . . así. . . . asi que no pierda su cita del día veintiseis.*
			(Okay? And we'll let Dr. Jacob know . . . so . . . don't miss your appointment on the 26th.)
9	P	▶	*Ah . . . muy bien . . . gracias.*
			(Oh . . . all right . . . thank you.)
10	HI	▶	*¿Okay Gimena?*
11	P	▶	*Muy amable, hasta luego . . . gracias.*
			(It's very kind of you . . . bye now . . . thank you.)
12	HI	▶	*Gracias y que le vaya bien . . . Okay Sarah?*
			(Thank you and I wish you well . . .)
13	M	▶	Okay . . . thank you . . . bye.
14	HI	▶	Bye bye.
15	M	▶	Bye.

The clerk explains why it is important to keep the appointment (turns 1, 3), and that no other solutions are possible. The clerk is coming to the end of the exchange but does not say goodbye to the patient. Consuelo says goodbye to the patient (turn 12) and ends the conversation. How does Consuelo construct that? She explains to the patient that it is important to keep the appointment (turns 4, 6, 8). Consuelo verifies the patient's comprehension once again (turn 10). The patient expresses appreciation for Consuelo's help and says goodbye to her (turn 11). Consuelo says goodbye (turn 12) and wishes the patient well. Only after closing the conversation with the patient does Consuelo return her attention to the clerk and close the interaction between them (turns 13–15). Consuelo chooses not to interpret her interaction with the patient to the clerk, but instead to close the ICE on her own. The choices that interpreters make are major indications of their role in the interaction.

Segment 5 illustrates several points about interpreters' ownership in closing ICEs. Firstly, interpreters at CH almost always create the lines to say goodbye. As we noted before, while HCPs only close the ICE by saying thank you and goodbye, interpreters constantly express their solidarity with patients by wishing them well. In this example, solidarity is coupled with affect (figure 3), as Consuelo expresses her care for the patient by reminding her three times of how important it is to not miss her appointment. Secondly, interpreters often take the initiative not only in the wording of the line but also in the actual utterance of the line, and then they report to the other party once it is done. This is demonstrated at turn 12.

Segment 6 illustrates another example of an interpreter who closes the ICE on her own initiative. In this ICE, Mariana (whom we encountered in segment 3) is facilitating an eleven-minute conversation between an English-speaking female nurse (N) and a Spanish-speaking male patient (P). The ICE is coming to an end.

Segment 6: Mariana (Tape 26: 187–196)
1   N   OK, that's all then, thank you.
2   HI ▶   OK Lisa, thank you. *Gracias señor, buen día y buena suerte.*
              (Thank you sir. Have a good day and good luck to you.)
3   P ▶   *A usted, muchas gracias, muy agradecido eh.*
              (Thank you. I appreciate it.)
4   HI ▶   Bye bye.
5   N ▶   Bye.

We see once again as in the previous two segments (4 and 5) that the nurse does not give the closing line (turn 2) to the interpreter. The patient responds by wishing the interpreter well (turn 3) and by addressing her directly. Mariana could have simply told the patient, "that is all sir" (turn 1), but instead, she chooses to follow the rules of politeness from the patient's culture, and closes the ICE accordingly. The nurse does not give those lines to her; Mariana is the owner. Like Marcos in segment 4, Mariana acts upon the system of categories (Brewer 1988 in chapter 3) that she developed for both parties, which results in her creation of a closing that satisfies the expectations that the patient has based on his cultural norms.

This analysis of openings and closings shows that interpreters begin and end ICEs using their own lines, not the lines given to them by the other interlocutors. In doing so, it seems that the cultural norms of politeness supersede those that transpire from the institutional power. In spite of the fact that HCPs may be in a hurry, or that the institution requires them to rush from one appointment to another, interpreters take time to close the interaction, ending it in a way that is acceptable to the Spanish speakers with whom they are interacting. It seems that the impressions they have formed trigger a categorization (Brewer 1988 in chapter 3) which leads to the expression of solidarity and affect. This occurred frequently during my twenty-two months of observation. Interpreters take ownership in ending the relationships that they constructed during the ICEs.

Major visibility: interpreters as owners of text

At CH, major visibility (which is highly consequential, since it impacts on the medical and personal information transmitted) does not occur during openings and closings (i.e. phases 1 [relating to patient] or 6 [terminating] of the medical interview). Rather, it occurs during phases 2 to 5 (i.e. during the discovery, the examination, the consideration of the condition, and the detailing of the treatment or of the further investigation). Following Hymes' taxonomy, we can see how the goals of the participants within an ICE during these phases differ significantly. The patient needs to get medical help, the HCP wants to provide the patient with her technical knowledge and expertise, and the interpreter must help the parties accomplish the communicative goals of the ICE.

The goals of the parties involved in the ICE are not the only elements that differ. Each participant brings his/her own set of expectations to the encounter as well. Patients expect to be listened to, HCPs expect to obtain the information necessary in order to make a diagnosis and present therapeutic options, and interpreters expect to help the monolingual parties communicate with one another. Sometimes patients arrive at a medical consult terrified because they feel poorly. They lack the linguistic repertoire (technical jargon, medicalese) to interact with the HCP, but they desperately want a solution. Sometimes HCPs are pressed for time, they do not have the linguistic repertoire to address the patients in lay terms, or they are not familiar with the patient's culture. It is up to interpreters to organize and coordinate these sets of resources, goals, and expectations. Interpreters have a list of orchestrations to carry out. Their performance as text owners is difficult because of the complexity of the ICE of which they are a part.

In the following sections, I look at bodies of ICEs at CH. Each of the ICEs presents at least one problem: as we have seen in chapter 3, the two monolingual participants share neither the same channels nor the same goals, expectations, forms of speech, norms of interaction or norms of interpreting. Sometimes, the requested message in an ICE does not get delivered. Interpreters coordinate moves towards consensual, collective agreement. While orchestrating these moves, the interpreter becomes part of the common voice, generally, between questions and answers. Because the parties that need to ask the questions and provide the answers cannot talk to one another using the same channels as speakers who share a language, they need a third interlocutor to orchestrate the conversation (the interpreter).

The interpreter exercises agency to achieve the communicative goals of the parties involved, playing a very active role. But, what is that role, what triggers it, and where does it get enacted?

The interpreter orchestrates communication between the parties in an ICE, and in doing so takes ownership of the text. This means that the interpreter exhibits some degree of visibility in every medical encounter. This visibility may be higher in some ICEs and lower in others, but seldom do interpreters produce closed renditions (Wadensjö 1998). More commonly they expand the renditions, producing text they own, based on the interplay of social factors affecting the encounter. Interpreters are powerful, visible parties that exercise agency to a higher or lesser degree. They perform in the openings, the closings, and the middles of the ICEs at CH. The following examples demonstrate a higher level of visibility than the openings and closings we have seen thus far, especially in terms of the amount of text ownership that interpreters produce, and in terms of their agency in orchestrating the dialogue. In exercising agency, interpreters have an impact on the relationship between HCP and patient characterized as informative, facilitative, responsive, and participatory (chapter 2).

Segment 7 demonstrates how Elda (whom we encountered in segment 2) helps a female Mexican patient communicate with a Caucasian male doctor about the patient's response to a treatment. The doctor, looking for a yes or no answer, wants to know if the new medication is helping the patient. The patient begins to tell a story. Elda interrupts her (turn 4) and asks for the yes or no answer. When the doctor hears the Spanish word *mejor*, he assumes that the medication is helping (turn 6). Elda manages the interaction by telling the doctor that the answer is still pending (turn 7) and asks the patient to answer the question. As the patient begins to overlap (turn 8), Elda takes control (turn 9) and explains the interaction traffic rules to the patient.

Segment 7: Elda (Tape 28: 000–140)

1	D	. . . so it helps you or it doesn't?
2	HI	*¿Le ayuda o no señora?*
		(Does it help you or not?)
3	P	[*No, pos, no es . . . Me pega fuerte y*
		(No . . . well . . . it is not . . . it is painful and . . .)
4 ▶	HI	[*¿Pero, le sirve?*
		(But, does it help you?)
5	P	[*Tantito*
		estaba mejor pero esta mañana . . .
		(Earlier I was feeling a little better, but this morning . . .)
6	D	It does help her, then?
7 ▶	HI	She is not answering my question, doctor. *¿Señora por qué no me dice si le ayuda o no el medicamento?*
		(Why don't you tell me if the medicine helps you or not?)
8	P	[*Es que . . . como le digo . . . si no camino . . .*
		(Well . . . how can I explain it . . . if I don't walk . . .)
9 ▶	HI	[*Señora espéreme un momentito ¡eh! Vamos a hacer una cosa cuando yo le hable, usted se queda callada y después usted habla y yo la escucho, sino no se puede y no nos entendemos.*
		(Ma'am hold on here . . . We are going to do the following: when I talk, you stay quiet and when you talk I listen. Otherwise it's impossible and we don't understand each other.)

This segment exemplifies how Elda claims ownership of text when she explores answers to the question, and she controls the flow of traffic by exercising power in the interaction. As Elda orchestrates moves, she produces text that is not given to her but that she considers necessary to continue to coordinate moves. For the utterance in turn 9, we need to look beyond the concept of expanded rendition in interaction-oriented interpreter initiative (Wadensjö 1998: 106–10). The doctor never actually produces an utterance to discipline the patient based on sociolinguistic rules of no overlapping. Elda knows that overlapping is the rule in Spanish, but she also knows that the doctor needs the information he is requesting, not the story that the patient begins to tell. To provide the doctor with the medical information that is essential, Elda tries to focus the patient on the effect of the medication, ignoring the story, and finally deciding to reprimand the patient. She exercises her power to control the traffic of communication and to lay down the rules. She thus impacts on the participatory and responsive nature of the doctor–patient relationship (chapter 2). This should not be construed as the interpreter's fault or responsibility. We may infer from this segment that Elda intervenes in response to the doctor's need to find out the yes or no answer. Turn 1 is not the first time the doctor inquires about the effects of the new medication. Two earlier attempts have failed, which explains the reasoning behind the reiteration of the question, looking just for a yes or no answer. The patient cannot tell her story if she is asked to answer yes or no, she cannot fully participate in history-taking, and the rapport building is compromised. We see in this segment how the interaction cannot escape the constraints that the institution (Bourdieu 1977 in chapter 3) imposes upon it and how Elda's behaviors are affected by these constraints. The doctor is pressed for time, holds a position of power, enjoys higher status (Webster and Foschi 1998 in chapter 3), and directs the line of questioning. Elda follows his lead, not that of the patient.

In the next segment, Annette (HI) interprets for a male Caucasian doctor and a female Mexican patient. During the interview, the doctor asks if the patient has been tested for tuberculosis (TB) (turn 4). Annette interprets this question for the patient (turn 5). The patient says that she had some tests done at one time, but she does not know if the tests were for TB (turn 6). Annette then explains to her (turn 7) what a TB test is and how it is performed, to see whether the patient has had one or not. Once Annette gets an answer from the patient, she reports back to doctor, and she also explains to the doctor what she has just said to the patient (turn 9).

Segment 8: Annette (Tape: 6 Call 2)

1	D	Let's see . . . no heart disease runs in the family, right?
2	HI	*Y no hay enfermedades del corazón que andan (sic) en la familia de usted, ¿verdad?* (No heart disease running in your family, right?)
3	P	No.
4	D	Has she ever been checked for the skin test for tuberculosis?
5 ▶	HI	*¿Le han hecho alguna vez el estudio de piel para tuberculosis?* (Have you ever been tested with the skin test for tuberculosis?)

6 ▶   P   *Pues, allá me hicieron estudios pero no sé si es para eso . . .*
              (Well, I had some tests done there, but I don't know if they were to
              check that . . .)
7 ▶   HI   *Es una aguja que se le meta (sic), le inyecta un poco (sic) líquido
              bajo la piel y tiene que regresar dentro de dos o tres días para que le
              (sic) vean si se ha cambiado (sic) la piel.*
              (It is a needle that is inserts (sic), it injects a little a (sic) liquid under
              the skin and you have to go back in two or three days so that they can
              see you (sic) if you (sic) have changed your skin.)
8   P   No.
9 ▶   HI   No, she hasn't had that. I just described for her what it was as she said
              she's had different tests but she wasn't sure if she has had
              tuberculosis, so I explained to her how PPD works.

At turn 6 Annette realizes that the patient does not know what the TB test
is. She explains it to the patient as she explores an answer. When asked about
this explanation in a follow-up interview, Annette refers to the patient's level of
education, saying that she could tell from the way they speak, that they are not
understanding. When this happens, she tailors her speech to theirs. Based on her
impressions (Brewer 1988 in chapter 3) of the patient's social status and level
of education, coupled with her ethnicity, Annette anticipates that the patient
may have problems understanding her. She performs comprehension checks
periodically and even asks patients to let her know if they have any problem
understanding her (she is aware of the fact that she is a non-native speaker of
Spanish and that the variety of Spanish she uses may be different from that
of the patient). In doing this, she exercises agency. In this segment, Annette,
on her own initiative, explained to the patient what a TB test is and how it
is performed. She says that taking initiative does not interfere with the trust-
building process that she establishes between herself and the doctor. Annette is
conscious of the fact that she is not involving the doctor in the steps she takes
to find the answer to his question (turns 5 to 8). Because she wants the doctor
to know what she is doing, Annette explains it to him after the fact (turn 9).
Annette orchestrates the brokering of comprehension with the exploring for
the answer and the building of trust. In orchestrating these moves, Annette
is the owner of her own lines. By supplying this information to the patient,
she impacts on the nature of the doctor–patient relationship. She replaces the
doctor in constructing an informative interaction, one of the characteristics of a
relationship-centered visit (chapter 2). For me, as an observer of this interpreted
encounter, the relationship seemed to be developing between Annette and the
patient.

Slowly moving up the visibility scale, the next segment finds Julio (HI)
interpreting for a Caucasian nurse (N) in ambulatory surgery and a four-year-
old Hispanic male, accompanied by his Spanish-speaking parents (P). During
the pre-operative period, the nurse comes across a consent form that is written

in Spanish. Since she cannot understand the language, and the parents cannot understand the medical terminology, the nurse solicits Julio's help. The form has been signed without witnesses, and now the nurse needs one of the parents to sign the form, and she will sign as a witness. Then, the nurse goes over the pre-operative instructions with the parents.

Segment 9: Julio (Tape 3: 118–134)

1	N	His surgery time is for eight thirty January twentieth he needs to be here on time. . . if he is going to be late he needs to call us . . . our phone number is five five five one two three four and let us know he's going to be late or is gonna cancel.
2	HI ▶	Are you going to give him a copy of the number?
3	N	Yes . . . the cop . . . the number is right here . . . it's . . .
4	HI	Okay.
5	N	In the . . .
6	HI	*Okay, miren caso de que no pudiera llegar el veinte a las ocho y media por alguna razón . . . por favor llame usted a ese número . . .* (Listen . . . in case you can't come on the twentieth at eight thirty for any reason . . . please call this number . . .)
7	P	Okay.
8	HI	*. . . que está indicando ella.* (. . . that she is indicating.)
9	P	Okay.
10	N	Okay? . . . and just let him be aware that we are a trauma center and although his son's surgery time or registration time is for eight thirty that morning . . . that doesn't necessarily mean his . . . son is going to have surgery at that time.
11	HI ▶	*A veces señor ocurren emergencias.* (Sometimes, emergencies happen.)
12	P ▶	*Ajá.* (Aha.)
13	HI ▶	*Entonces no siempre es con seguridad que le vayan a hacer la operación a esa hora . . .* (So it's not always certain that surgery will take place at that time . . .)
14	P	Okay.
15	HI ▶	*Está programada por ahora a esa hora.* (For now, it is programmed for that time.)
16	P ▶	[*Las ocho y media . . . pero puede surgir algún problema que lo pasen más tarde.* (Eight thirty . . . but should a problem arise, they will schedule it for later.)
17	HI ▶	*Así es.* (That's right.)
18	P ▶	Okay.
19	N	Okay? Does he have any other questions?
20	HI	*¿Tiene alguna otra pregunta señor?* (Any other questions?)

21	P	*No . . . nada más.*
		(No . . . nothing else.)
22	N ▶	Okay . . . um . . . can you please sign and date this . . . hm . . . pre-op instruction form? And I'll give him a copy of these instructions.
23	HI ▶	*Firme ahi por favor y ahorita le da la copia eh . . . No le vaya a dar ni dulce ni . . . ni . . . ni goma de mascar . . . absolutamente nada . . . eh?*
		(Sign there please and she's going to give you the copy . . . Don't give him any candy . . . or chewing gum . . . absolutely nothing . . . okay?)
24	P	Okay.
25	HI ▶	*¿No tiene dientes flojos?*
		(No loose teeth?)
26	P	No.
27	N	No more questions?
28	HI	*¿Tiene alguna pregunta?*
		(Any other questions?)
29	P	No.

In this segment, Julio starts claiming ownership when he asks the nurse if she is going to give a copy of the form to the father (turn 3). The nurse then uses one turn to explain the fact that surgery times are not exact, because of the nature of a trauma center (turn 10). The interpreting of that utterance gets orchestrated in seven turns between Julio and the patient (turns 11–18). Julio makes sure that the parent is following him by pausing and waiting for the parent's acknowledgment (turns 11–15). The parent gets to summarize the idea (turn 16), and Julio verifies the parent's understanding and then summarizes once again on turn 17. Once there are no more questions on the part of the parent, Julio, on his own initiative, advises the parent not to let his son have any candy or chewing gum (turn 23). This line was not given to him by the nurse. Additionally, Julio asks if the patient has any loose teeth (turn 25). The nurse verifies if there are any more questions to which the patient once again responds no. Julio has definitely added to the nurse's recommendations based on his previous knowledge of pre-operative instructions. Immediately after this assignment was over, Julio and I had a chance to talk. I asked him about the advice he gave to the patient, which did not come from the nurse. He explained that he draws from the experience he gained while working in the pediatric unit and from his experience as a father of three. Julio also explained to me that loose teeth can be problematic when the patient is intubated. Julio becomes visible in this segment by explaining things to the patient and verifying the patient's comprehension. In subsequent interviews with Julio, we discussed this issue. He said that many times, providers use fancy words (*palabras de domingo*) that he always simplifies or exemplifies for the patient. Like Annette, Julio takes it upon himself to broker comprehension for the patient, thus impacting on the informative and participatory nature of a relationship-centered encounter. We ask ourselves once again, which relationship gets constructed, the one between patient and nurse or the one between patient and interpreter? Like Annette, Marcos, and Mariana, Julio produces text that he owns, based on the interplay of social factors and institutional norms affecting the encounter. Julio is a father of three, and his parenthood plays out as he expresses solidarity with the patient's parents by giving them more information than they expect. This segment shows that Julio, like the other co-participants in the interaction, constructs a message out of the interplay of linguistic and social features and not just out of propositional context, independent of the interlocutors (Irvine 1992 in chapter 3). The propositional context uttered by the nurse in turn 22 (Okay . . . um . . . can you please sign and date this . . . hm . . . pre-op instruction form? And I'll give him a copy of these instructions) could not possibly result in the context present in the second part of turn 23 (Don't give him any candy . . . or chewing gum . . . absolutely nothing . . . okay?) or in turn 25 (no loose teeth?) if Julio were to merely language switch. These lines can only be explained on the basis of the social features to which Julio attends: parents need to be given this advice, and during this interview they did not receive it from the nurse. Consequently, he takes it upon himself to make up for it.

In the next segment, Rogelio (HI) is interpreting between a female Caucasian medical admitting clerk (M) and a female Hispanic patient (P). The patient has called CH to make a return appointment with her regular doctor. She would also like to be seen as soon as possible for head and neck pain. The clerk is scheduling an appointment with the patient's regular doctor and is also calling the urgent care clinic to inquire about the next available appointment. The clerk schedules the return appointment.

Segment 10: Rogelio (Tape 43, Call 6: 199–256)

1	M	. . . the return with Dr. Lopez is for May . . . the third . . .
2	HI	*¿Señora?*
		(Ma'am?)
3	P	*Mande.*
		(Yes.)
4	HI	*Tiene una cita con el doctor Lopez el tres de mayo.*
		(You have an appointment with doctor Lopez on May third.)
5	M	At ten forty five in the morning.
6	HI	*A las diez cuarenta y cinco.*
		(At ten forty five.)
7	P	Mmmm.
8	M	So . . . hold on and. . . . and I'll . . . call Urgent Care to get her appointment today, okay? Hold on please.
9	HI	*Y ahorita . . . le van a llamar a la clínica de urgencias para que le den cita hoy.*
		(And now . . . they are going to call Urgent Care so that you get an appointment today.)
10	P	Hmmm.

11	HI	*Un momento, no cuelgue.*
		(Just a minute, don't hang up.)
12	P	*No, está bien.*
		(No, it's okay.)
13	M	Keep holding, okay? I am on hold with Mactum Urgent Care.
14	HI	[*¿Señora?*
		(Ma'am)
15	M	[Okay.
16	HI	[*No cuelgue señora.*
		(Don't hang up ma'am.)
17	M	[Thank you.
18	P ▶	*Oiga jov . . . oiga.*
		(Listen youn . . . [young man] listen.)
19	HI ▶	*Dígame.*
		(Yes.)
20	P ▶	*¿Cuándo me dijo que pa' Mayo? (02) No: (02) que no tenía pluma.*
		(When in May did you tell me? No: . . . I didn't have a pen.)
21	HI ▶	*No, no haga eso . . . repítame cuando no . . . cuando no sienta que la tiene . . . ahorita le pregunto otra vez.*
		(No, don't do that . . . repeat it to me when you don't . . . when you don't think you have one . . . now I am going to ask her again.)
22	P	(laugh) *Sí, está bien.*
		(Yes, it's fine.)
23	HI ▶	*Es el tres de mayo.*
		(It's on May third.)
24	P	*Ah . . . el tres de mayo . . . ajá . . .*
		(Oh . . . on May third . . . aha.)
25	HI ▶	*Yo me acuerdo que era porque pensé que era el día de la Santa Cruz . . . tres de mayo.*
		(I remember because I thought that it was on the day of the Holy Cross . . . May third.)
26	P	*Ah . . . tres . . . ajá.*
		(Oh . . . third . . . aha.)
27	HI	*Pero la hora creo que . . . ¿apuntó la hora?*
		(But the time I think . . . did you write down the time?)
28	P	*A las . . . diez . . . ¿no?*
		(At . . . ten . . . right?)
29	HI	*¿Diez? . . . ahorita le preguntamos.*
		(Ten? Now we'll ask her.)
30	P	*Sí . . . está bien . . . ajá.*
		(Yes . . . it's fine . . . aha.)

The patient does not remember the date of the appointment, so she requests repetition from Rogelio (turns 18/20), rather than from the medical admitting clerk. On his own initiative, Rogelio light-heartedly reprimands the patient for not writing down the date and time, by using a rising tone (turn 21) that causes the patient to laugh (turn 22). At turn 21, Rogelio changes his reprimanding tone and advises the patient on what to do next time if she does not have a pen handy. He also offers to ask the clerk for the appointment date. Rogelio does not ask the clerk, but rather he gives it to the patient (turn 23). He remembers associating the date with a religious celebration (turn 25). The segment finishes with Rogelio not giving the patient the time of the appointment, because he cannot remember it (turn 29). Interestingly, in line 15, the clerk puts the conversation on hold. Rogelio and the patient continue the interaction on their own from turns 18 to 30, and then the clerk rejoins the conversation. These twelve turns cannot be explained on the basis of expanded renditions or interpreter-interaction-oriented initiatives (Wadensjö 1998), since the interpreter has no original on which to expand and is not concerned about the flow of the talk. The interpreter's trigger to intervene and hold the conversation may be explained by considering the interplay of the interpreter's and the patient's social realities. Triggered by solidarity towards the patient, Rogelio first gently exercises power to reprimand the patient. Then, he moves into an advising mode. After that, he expresses solidarity once again, both by giving the patient the date and by not giving him the time (because he is unsure of the time). In subsequent conversations I had with Rogelio about this transcript, he noted that he generally overprotects patients, and while he does not want to patronize the patients, he is conscious of the fact that they are not meticulous in keeping track of their appointments and their own health-related issues. He believes that it is up to him to teach them to write things down and to be careful. He perceives differences in levels of education among patients and he decides which ones need extra help from him. Therefore in this segment we see that Rogelio's categorization (Brewer 1988 in chapter 3) of patients and his decision on what patients can and cannot do (Fiske and Taylor 1991 in chapter 3), coupled with his own experiential knowledge (Duranti 1992 in chapter 3) trigger his reactions.

In the next segment (segment 11), Vicente (HI) interprets for a female Caucasian nurse and a Mexican female patient. We join them during history-taking. The nurse wants to know whether the patient suffers from any chronic illnesses. She does not ask the questions for Vicente to interpret. Rather, she asks Vicente to produce the line of questioning (turn 1). In carrying out the nurse's request, Vicente adopts a series of strategies that render him more visible in the interaction.

		Segment 11: Vicente (Tape 17, Call 3: 200–224)
1	N	Can you ask her about chronic illnesses, diabetes . . . all that?
2 ▶	HI	*Ahá. Señora Mesa ¿alguna vez dijo el doctor, aunque sea veinte años atrás, aquí o allá, que tenía usted diabetes?*
		(Mrs. Mesa, has a doctor ever told you even twenty years ago here or there that you had diabetes?)
3	P	No.

4 ▶	HI	*¿Que tenía la presión alta?*
		(That you had high blood pressure?)
5	P	No.
6 ▶	HI	*¿Que tenía alguna enfermedad al corazón?*
		(That you had heart disease?)
7	P	Noooo.
8 ▶	HI	*¿Que era enferma del hígado? ¿De los riñones? ¿Del estómago?*
		(That you suffered from liver problems? Kidney problems? Stomach problems?)
9	P	No.
10 ▶	HI	*¿Alguna vez la operaron, la internaron? ¿Allá o aquí?*
		(Have you ever been operated on or hospitalized? Here or there?)
11	P	Noooo.
12 ▶	HI	*¿Nunca ha estado usted enferma?*
		(You have never been sick?)
13	P	*Esteeee si estuve enferma pero . . . es deeee depresión nerviosa, no de otra cosa.*
		(Well . . . I was sick but. . . . it was de . . . nervous depression . . . I did not suffer from anything else.)
14 ▶	HI	*Okay . . . ¿y la internaron por la depresión nerviosa?*
		(Okay, and were you hospitalized for nervous depression?)
15	P	*Sí . . .*
		(Yes.)
16	HI	*¿Allá o aquí?*
		(Over there or here?)
17	P	*Esteee . . . emmm . . . en Azusa . . .*
		(Hmmm . . . in Azusa . . .)
18	HI	*¿En dónde?*
		(Where?)
19	P	*Azusa . . . cerca de Los Angeles.*
		(In Azusa, near Los Angeles.)
20 ▶	HI	Ya . . . she is saying that she denies diabetes, denies cardiovascular disease, denies blood pressure, denies eh . . . problems with her stomach and her liver . . . she said that she was . . . denies surgery . . . she was admitted once eh . . . close to Los Angeles . . . ehmm . . . for depression.
21	N	Okay . . . but she does not take any medicine now?
22 ▶	HI	*Señora ¿está usted tomando alguna medicina estos días?*
		(Ma'am, are you taking any medicine these days?)
23	P	No.
24 ▶	HI	*¿Alguna medicina que compró sin receta?*
		(Any over-the-counter medicine?)
25	P	No.
26 ▶	HI	*¿Que trajo de allá, que le dio la comadre Juana?*
		(That you brought from there, that Comadre[3] Juana gave to you?)

---

[3] In some Spanish-speaking areas, the term *comadre* refers to a woman's close friend who is often also the godmother of her child.

27	P	*No, nada.*
		(No, nothing.)
28 ▶	HI	Negative . . . negative.
29	N	Okay, all right . . . sounds just like she has the blues . . . her lungs are clear, she is breathing fine and her color looks good I'm gonna check her oxygen saturation and then probably send her home with advice and give her the number to call . . .
30	HI	*Okay . . . Señora dice nuestra enfer . . .*
		[
		(Okay . . . our nurse says . . .
31	N	[I'll be right back . . .
32	HI	*[mera que le ha escuchado los pulmones y suenan bien . . .*
		(that she has heard your lungs and they are fine . . .)
33 ▶	P	*Sííí.*
		(Yeees.)
34	HI	*Dice que su color está bien . . . que . . . le va a medir el oxígeno de la sangre.*
		(She says that your skin color looks fine . . . that . . . and that she will measure the oxygen in your blood.)
35 ▶	P	Okay.
36 ▶	HI	*Eso no duele . . . le va a poner una lucecita en uno de sus dedos solamente por un minuto y después la manda a su casa con unas recomendaciones.*
		(That doesn't hurt . . . and she will put a little light in one of your fingers for one minute and then she will send you home with advice.)
37	P	Okay.

Vicente starts by altering the register of chronic illnesses for the patient (turn 2). He gives examples of various chronic illnesses on turns 2, 4, 6, and 8. As he does this, he also asks where she was living during the time that any of these illnesses may have occurred (here or there, i.e. US or Mexico). When the nurse asks Vicente to ask the patient about chronic illnesses, she does not specify which illnesses she means. But, she did add "and all that" to "chronic illness" (by which she may have meant hospitalizations, surgeries, or medications). Adding "and all that" (turn 1) could be interpreted as a way of asking for the complete medical history. This latter interpretation would include the surgical and hospitalization questions (turns 10, 14, 16, and 18). Vicente asks about chronic illness and surgeries or hospitalizations. He chooses to do this, even though he could have chosen not to do it. Once he finishes, he reports back to the nurse on turn 20, summarizing his findings.

The nurse then asks a question (turn 21) about medications (which is part of the medical history), because she did not get that information after the first question. Vicente asks about medicine intake on turns 22, 24, and 26. He looks for information, not limited to the life of the patient in the US. He explores cultural references such as home remedies on the *comadre's* advice (turn 26), and he summarizes the information for the nurse on turn 28. On turn 29, the nurse states her findings and her plan for the patient. It takes Vicente eight turns (30 to 37) to orchestrate this statement with the patient. As Vicente explains the findings and the next step to the patient (30, 32, 34, and 36), he receives the patient's comments and feedback (33, 35, and 37) as he constructs his lines.

In this segment we see how Vicente uses different strategies to accomplish communicative goals. He slides messages down the register scale, investigates answers, expands and summarizes utterances, and brokers cultural references. He does all of this based on his perception of the patient. Vicente applies these strategies without a specific direction at the prompt "and all that." Vicente's role becomes visible as he orchestrates the talk. During informal interviews, I asked Vicente about these strategies and why he had used them. He explained to me that many times patients either do not understand the HCP's question or do not give the complete answer. He is convinced that his role involves brokering the questions in a way that patients will understand, and also digging and digging until he obtains the information that is necessary to answer the question. Vicente takes it upon himself to create a patient-centered encounter and, once again, he replaces the provider in the relationship-centered medical visit. In this segment, it appears that what triggers Vicente's replacing of the provider (turns 2–20) in the line of questioning are two different factors. On the one hand, Vicente's training as a physician contributes to his habitus (Bourdieu 1977 in chapter 3) which in turn constrains his behaviors. Could it be that he has a higher level of comfort in creating this line of questioning because of his background in medicine? On the other hand, the nurse did authorize Vicente to ask about chronic illnesses. So, on the basis of social comparison theory (Festinger 1954 in chapter 3), could it be that the nurse's deferring to him (by considering him a socially oriented peer) empowers Vicente causing him to perceive that the nurse believes him to be up to the challenge? Additionally, by perceiving that the patient and the nurse do not belong to the same speech community (Hymes 1974 in chapter 3), Vicente takes it upon himself to broker the comprehension of this line of questioning by breaking it into smaller units and examples and by adding a cultural reference to the *comadre*.

In the next segment Joaquín (HI), whom we encountered in segment 1, interprets for a male Caucasian doctor and a female Mexican patient. During the interview phase, the doctor needs to find out more information about the patient's reported pain. We join their conversation at the point in which the doctor tells the interpreter to ask the patient to rate her pain on a scale from one to ten.

Segment 12: Joaquín (Tape 30, Call 1: 065–275)

1	D	In a scale from one to ten, how would she rate her pain?
2 ▶	HI	*A ver Señora Rita, en una escala de uno a diez ¿que número le pondría a su dolor? Por ejemplo, si el uno es que está para irse a bailar y no tiene nada y el diez es que se está muriendo, dónde estaría el dolor . . .*
		(Let's see Mrs. Rita, on a scale from one to ten, what number would you assign to your pain? For example, if one is a pain that would allow you to go dancing, you almost don't feel anything and ten is so painful that you are dying from that pain . . .)
3	P	*¿Cómo dice?*
		(What did you say?)
4	HI	*Qué . . . ¿qué número le daría a su dolor?*
		(What . . . what number would you give to your pain?)
5	P	*Pos . . . a mí me duele mucho.*
		(Well . . . it hurts a lot.)
6 ▶	HI	*¿Cuánto es mucho señora? ¿Mucho que se está muriendo del dolor?*
		(How much is a lot Ma'am? Does a lot mean you are dying from the pain?)
7	P	*Pos . . . no . . . muriendo no, pero . . .*
		(Well . . . no . . . not dying . . . but . . .)
8 ▶	HI	*¿Qué cosas puede hacer con el dolor?*
		(Which things can you do when you are in pain?)
9	P	*Pos no sé . . . cuando me duele mucho me siento.*
		(Well, I don't know . . . when it is very hard I sit down.)
10 ▶	HI	*Pero ¿puede cocinar con el dolor?*
		(But, can you cook when you are in pain?)
11	P	*A veces me pega fuerte y no.*
		(Sometimes it is very hard and I can't.)
12 ▶	HI	*Y, esas veces, ¿siente como que se va a morir o no tanto?*
		(And at times, does it feel like you are going to die or it is not so hard?)
13	P	*No, morir no, no más pega fuerte.*
		(No, not like I'm going to die, it's just hitting me hard.)
14 ▶	HI	*¿Le ponemos un ocho o un nueve?*
		(Do we give it an eight or a nine?)
15	P	*Pos yo no sé, pos sí . . .*
		(I don't know, yes . . .)
16 ▶	HI	When it is most painful it would be close to an eight, doctor.
17	D	Okay.

Joaquín takes fourteen turns (2–15) to broker the pain-rating scale, and what the numbers in the scale may mean to the patient. He asks the patient a number of questions, providing examples of activities that the patient may or may not be able to do when she experiences the pain. When the patient is still unable to rate her pain, Joaquín narrows the options to an eight or a nine (turn 14). The patient never does rate her pain accurately, but Joaquín reports to the doctor the rate that he suggested to the patient (turn 16).

The use of a scale to rate pain does not necessarily work in situations where the two communicating parties represent different cultures (i.e. the medical culture and the layperson's culture) and belong to two different speech communities (Hymes 1974 in chapter 3). Joaquín tries to bridge the gap between the doctor's and the patient's way of talking about pain, by making the numbers more concrete for the patient. He expands the scale ratings and provides the patient with some examples of activities that she may or may not be able to do when she is in pain. In doing this he creates text, and then he goes beyond expanding a rendition, to almost provide an answer. We see in Joaquín, as in all the other interpreters, instances of expanded renditions (Wadensjö 1998) triggered by social factors. He summarizes the patient's comprehension (or lack thereof) into a rating that the patient never actually produced. Joaquín not only orchestrates the moves to produce the rate, but he also replaces the monolingual patient by producing it. Joaquín replaces the provider to broker a pain scale and he replaces the patient in giving a rating. In doing this, Joaquín seems to be fully participating in this relationship-centered interview, which ends up being between the patient and him and the doctor and him. During my informal interviews with Joaquín, we discussed examples in which he brokers comprehension for the patients, and the responsibility that goes along with inferring answers from the patient (in helping patients construct them). Joaquín is aware of this responsibility and believes it is part of his job. Through the lens of linguistic anthropology, we can explore how Joaquin assumes his share of social responsibility in constructing talk (Duranti 1992 in chapter 3). The meaning of the pain scale is not objective; the ratings on it depend on how the parties construe them. The scale needs to be understood, and Joaquín feels responsible for making this happen.

In the next segment, Mauro (HI) interprets for a Hispanic female patient (P), the patient's landlady (W), and a Caucasian female nurse (N). The patient calls CH, because she is not feeling well. She reports shortness of breath and pain, as well as allergies and a runny nose. During history-taking, the nurse focuses on the shortness of breath. The patient reports that the condition is accompanied by chest pain that irradiates into her jaw, arm, and back. In light of the symptoms, the nurse focuses on the possibility of a heart attack and suggests that the patient call 911. The patient denies the severity of the case and does not want to call the paramedics, because she cannot afford the expense. She is hoping to get an appointment with a doctor at CH.

Segment 13: Mauro (Tape 55: 237–414)

1   P   *Entonces no me dan cita para allá.*
               (So you don't give me an appointment to go there.)

2   HI ▶   *Señora . . .*
              (Ma'am . . .)
3   P   Hmmm.
4   HI ▶   *Llámele a los paramédicos . . . al nueve uno uno . . . okay señora?*
              (Call the paramedics . . . at nine one one . . . okay Ma'am?)
5   P   [*Bueno*
              (All right)
6   N ▶   [Mauro, ask her
              who else is in her house.
7   HI   *¿Quién más está en su casa señora?*
              (Who else is in your house Ma'am?)
8   P   *Ehm . . . una señora que . . . que vive . . . porque yo rento un*
              cuarto . . . aquí a una señora.
              (Hmm . . . a woman that . . . that lives here . . . because I rent a
              room . . . here from this woman.)
9   HI ▶   She is renting one of the . . . . rooms in the house . . . hmm . . . do you
              want to speak to the other woman?
10 N   Yeah . . . let's try to talk to someone else.
11 HI   *Señora . . . déjeme hablar con la persona que está con usted.*
              (Let me speak with the person that is with you.)
12 P   *A ver . . . permítame*
              (Let's see . . . excuse me . . .)
13 HI   Hmmmhmmm.
              (While the patient puts the other woman on the line, Mauro and the
              nurse talk about denial of the patient and how classic this denial is.
              They also discuss how busy last night was at the hospital and if the
              service had to call for extra help.)
14 W   *Bueno.*
              (Hello)
15 HI   *A ver . . .*
              (Let's see here . . .)
16 N   [Does this lady speak English?
17 HI   [*¿Usted habla inglés?*
              (Do you speak English?)
18 W   *No* (nurse laughs).
19 HI ▶   *Mire señorita . . . este:*
              (Look miss . . . ah)
20 W   [*Señora*
              (Mrs.)
21 HI ▶   *Señora . . . está hablando con Mary, una de las enfermeras de aquí*
              del condado. Mi nombre es Mauro Sanchez, yo soy uno de los
              intérpretes del condado. La situación de la señora Fernandez es que
              pensamos que la señora tiene un estee . . . tenga un infarto.
              (You are speaking with Mary, one of the county nurses. My name is
              Mauro Sanchez, I am one of the county interpreters. The situation
              with Mrs. Fernandez is that we think that she has a . . . may have a
              heart attack.)

22   W   *[No . . . o sea que ella sí*
camina bien . . . nada más quería checar.
(No . . . I mean she is able to walk fine . . . she only wanted to
check.)

23   HI ▶   *[No, no. Escuche.*
(No, no, listen.)

24   W   *¡Oh!*

25   HI ▶   *Escuche . . . queremos que le llamen al nueve uno uno para que*
vengan los paramédicos y la revisen . . . que ellos determinen si
efectivamente tiene un infarto al corazón o no. ¿Okay? . . . pero
antes que haga cualquier cosa llame al nueve uno uno para que
vengan a revisarla.
(Listen . . . we want you to call nine one one, so that the paramedics
can come check her . . . they can determine if she is indeed having a
heart attack or not, okay? But before doing anything else, call nine
one one so that they come to check her.)

26   W   *[Ah . . . bueno*
(Oh . . . okay)

27   HI   *Si no tiene un infarto, qué bien ¿verdad?*
(If she doesn't have a heart attack, that is great, right?)

28   W   *[Mhm*

29   HI   *Pero hay que . . . los síntomas que está dando la señora son muy*
compatibles con un infarto . . .
(But you have to . . . the symptoms that she is describing are very
compatible with a heart attack . . .)

30   W   *Síi.*
(Yees.)

31   HI   *¿Okay?*

32   W   *Ajá.*
(Aha.)

33   HI ▶   Okay so I told her the situation and we are trying to encourage her
to . . . have her call nine one one.

34   N   All right, okay, thanks Mauro, okay, bye bye.

35   HI   *Hasta luego.*
(Bye.)

We see a higher degree of visibility in this segment as Mauro replaces both
the nurse and the patient. He explains to the patient that she needs to call the
paramedics right away (turns 2–4), while she insists on going to the clinic.
Then, when the nurse asks who else is there in the house (turn 6), Mauro finds
out and then suggests that the nurse speak with the other woman (turn 9). When
the nurse realizes that the woman does not speak English, she temporarily
withdraws from the interaction and Mauro replaces her (turns 21–33). He tells
the woman that she is speaking with the nurse (turn 21), introduces himself
as an interpreter, and then continues with the conversation without reporting

back to the nurse. Once the interaction is over, he summarizes it for the nurse at turn 33. In this delicate situation, time is precious, and the responsibility is enormous. Mauro orchestrates the moves and takes ownership of the text. In doing this, he replaces the monolingual interlocutor almost completely, thus taking on this tremendous responsibility. He also alters the nature of the HCP–patient relationship by undertaking the informative, facilitative and responsive approach all by himself. When asked about this responsibility, Mauro explains that his role varies from one ICE to another. In some instances he can afford to be more patient than in others. In this particular case, the sense of urgency is clear, and the patient does not understand the consequences of non-compliance, which prompts Mauro to be hard on the patient in order to convey the severity of the situation. Although he works as an interpreter, Mauro's background as a physician is (as in the case of Vicente, segment 11) an undeniable part of his habitus (Bourdieu 1977 in chapter 3). This may explain why the sense of emergency is so clear to him. His training as a physician may socially orient him more with the nurse (Festinger 1954 in chapter 3), since they share a discourse community (Hymes 1974 in chapter 3) and the opinion that the patient is in denial about the possibility of a heart attack.

The preceding seven segments illustrate the higher degrees of visibility, which occur in places other than openings and closings. This visibility is highly consequential, *vis à vis* the medical and personal information transmitted as well as to the nature of the relationship-centered encounter. Visibility is evidenced by the following behaviors on the part of the interpreters: exploring answers, expanding and summarizing statements, brokering comprehension and explaining technical terms, bridging cultural gaps, expressing affect, and replacing interlocutors. As the interpreter becomes the owner of text, visibility increases. When this happens, the interpreter's role is highly consequential, as we have seen in segments 7 through 13. Triggered by social factors, the interpreter gradually claims more ownership of the text, and impacts on the medical or personal information that is exchanged during the ICE and the provider–patient relationship.

ICEs at CH are complex. A Hymesian approach to the medical ICE demonstrates that any ICE differs from a monolingual communicative event at the hospital. Medical ICEs also differ from those in other settings (such as the courts). When interpreters at CH participate in the ICE, they are visible. As we have seen, openings and closings (which are in essence highly ritualized) show minor visibility instances, in which there is an occasional involvement of the interpreter as owner of the text. We have also seen instances of major visibility, where the interpreter, triggered by the interplay of social factors, gradually replaces the monolingual interlocutor by becoming owner of the text.

In this chapter we witnessed interpreters orchestrating moves and coordinating information-based relations between speakers. In the examples presented, we saw interpreters attending simultaneously to structural, cultural, interactional, and linguistic difficulties. They constantly balance how to talk and how not to talk about things. In being visible, interpreters simultaneously attend to a variety of relations that probably can be best described by Becker's definition of contextual interpretation of text (1995: 186). According to Becker, interpreters attend to:

- Structural relations, because they relate parts of the text at hand with the whole. In segment 7 turn 9, for example, we saw how Elda was relating the stories told by the patient to the question of whether or not the new medicine was helping. Interpreters permanently engage in relating an answer or a comment to the problem at hand.
- Generic relations, as they relate text to prior text. When patients tell stories and doctors impatiently press for yes or no answers, interpreters engage in generic relations to meet both parties' needs. In the same segment (segment 7), Elda (turn 7) relates the doctor's question (turn 6) to another one he had previously asked (turn 1).
- Medial relations, as they relate the text to the medium by which it is produced. If interlocutors produce text based on an x-ray film, a report or a scale, interpreters relate the text to those media, which are not text. This is demonstrated in segment 10, when Joaquín brokered the scale used to rate pain.
- Interpersonal relations, as they relate text to participants in a text act. Interpreters engage in making text more accessible to participants or in limiting text to participants' needs. In segment 8, Annette's explanation of the TB test, first to the patient (turn 7) and then to the doctor (turn 9), is an illustration of this interpersonal relation of text to participants.
- Referential relations, as they relate text to nature and to the world that lies beyond language. Participants come from different worlds and worldviews. Interpreters treat text in reference to those. In segment 11, Vicente illustrates this by referring the questions that the doctor is asking the patient to "here or there" (turns 2, 10, or 26) or by incorporating natural herbs prescribed by the *comadre* and over-the-counter medicine to the concept of medicine used by the doctor.
- Silential relations, as they relate the text to the unspoken and the unspeakable. Interpreters work within silences; they interpret silences, and they cause silences. They fill the silence of the others. In segment 9, when the patient states that he has no more questions (turn 21) Julio fills the silence by giving the patient extra advice. Julio explains that he should not give any chewing gum to the boy (turn 23) and elicits information about loose teeth (turn 25).

At the beginning of this chapter, Becker refers to translation as the first step to understand a message that is distant to us. Translation (and interpreting in this particular case) opens up for us a new way of looking at cross-cultural communication in a medical setting. At CH we have now seen how interpreters deal with their own exuberances and deficiencies in dealing with text, and the types of self-corrections they perform.

7   Interpreters' voices

In sorting out the puzzle of the role of interpreters during an ICE, a crucial piece of information is the interpreters' perception of their role. This emic perspective (Van Maanen 1988) allows us to triangulate the evidence of the role at play (discussed in the previous chapter) and the self-reported data obtained from the IPRI. This perspective made it possible for me to contextualize my observations on the role that interpreters play (chapter 6).

My conversations with the informants on their role were in the form of semi-structured interviews. As mentioned in chapter 4, I explored three issues during the interviews: (1) their perceptions of the parties with whom they work (patients and HCPs); (2) sources of stress and tension at work; and (3) their role. Each interview lasted approximately forty-five minutes.

In the following sections I synthesize my analysis of each interpreter's interview. During these interviews, the interpreters interjected anecdotes, stories, and examples, while the manager focused on the skills that are required of interpreters who work at CH. Of the eleven interviewees (ten interpreters and the manager), seven chose Spanish as the language for the interview and four chose English. For the sake of brevity in this chapter, most of the Spanish quotes are translated into English. Informants, except for the manager, are presented in alphabetical order.

Roberto, the manager

Roberto perceives the parties with whom he works as very different from one another: HCPs are educated and powerful, pressed for time, and in need of accurate information. Since he believes that meeting the needs of HCPs is the purpose of his job, Roberto feels that the interpreter should focus the patient on the answer required by the HCP. He perceives patients as less sophisticated; for him it is a challenge to get them to collaborate in meeting the HCPs' needs.

Roberto feels that the patients' lack of sophistication calls for linguistic adjustments on the part of the interpreters. He believes that it is up to the interpreters, during the first turns of an ICE, to diagnose the level of comprehension (i.e. education) of the patient and adjust the register accordingly. The importance of this task should not be underestimated, since a mistake could result in an insult to the patient or a prolongation of the medical encounter. For Roberto, the lack of sophistication on the part of the patients also surfaces with what he describes as an inability to comply. He explains:

Sometimes it's difficult to communicate with patients because they don't always follow your instructions. As an interpreter, you have to go almost like word by word . . . because you don't want to add or delete, or change. When you hear a question in English, like "How long have you been sick?" I say *"¿Por cuánto tiempo ha estado enfermo?"* (How long have you been sick?) Many times the patient does not answer the question. The patient starts saying: "Oh 20 years ago I was in an accident, and I hit my head, and I am having some problem here with my vision." And doctors don't want patients to do that. They want question and answer, you know brief. So, we have to focus the patient again, and say, "Señor, the question was, how long have you been sick this time."

The interpreter must find the most polite and accurate manner in which he can keep the patient on track while brokering the comprehension of linguistically sophisticated elements. When I asked Roberto to define what he looks for in prospective interpreters, he named accuracy as the most important element, but he also mentioned fluency in the working languages. Language ability is more important than cultural awareness for Roberto. In his opinion, cultural knowledge can be acquired on the job, but the language cannot. After language ability, the next requirement is knowledge of medical terminology, followed by memory and retention. He also mentions friendliness as an essential characteristic.

In Roberto's experience, qualified interpreters are hard to find. When he reflects on weaknesses of past candidates, he points to inaccuracy and incorrect grammar. He believes that the staff should monitor their own work more closely. Roberto bases his opinion of prospective interpreters on his ability to predict who is and who is not qualified to be an interpreter. He states:

You know, there are people who you look at and you say, oh this person can just learn. You know that already when you try. You know people who can work when you see them . . . but you see someone repeating the same thing. And you tell them twenty times. They're never going to change . . . because they don't put any effort into learning . . . or because they just can't learn.

Roberto contradicts himself when he tries to explain what he means by accurate and complete information, as he tells a story about a former employee:

And one of [the complaints] was that this person was not interpreting word-by-word, which we don't have to do. Sometimes it's because interpreters rearrange. You don't hear word-by-word. You just hear the total message. And it is true that many interpreters delete information. So many people just kind of summarize sometimes when it's a lot of information, and I think interpreters shouldn't delete anything. There are a lot of things that are not important. And it's not going to be a problem in communicating because sometimes you hear a lot of information that is not . . . going to be clear. If that is the case, I guess you can . . . do that. But many people don't understand that. They want to hear every single word.

Roberto and I discussed the training of interpreters at CH. When I referred to a specific set of skills, such as keeping the patient on track, coping with the challenges of HCPs who trust their high school Spanish more than the rendition of the interpreter, Roberto's opinion mirrors the literature; interpreting is a trade that can be learned by observation. He says:

. . . new interpreters . . . are doing this on the field. The interpreters who are . . . experienced . . . train [the new interpreters]. Because newcomers follow experienced interpreters, they listen to them before they themselves do any interpreting. When they are on the speakerphones, they plug an extra headset and listen. They [shadow] different interpreters to learn different styles. And then they come to my office and I go over [written material] . . . with them that they . . . have to read. And then we have . . . periodic meetings, where they can talk about the problems they are having, if any, how they deal with situations. There are a lot of issues they face, and so they have questions.

Interpreting, then, seems to be a craft or an art that is learned through shadowing, observation, and practice. Interestingly, there is a tension between Roberto's prescription of the interpreter's role ("just to interpret") and his description of what the staff does at IS. He explains how interpreters are team players with HCPs, assisting them beyond interpreting during ICEs. Roberto uses the cardiology stress test to illustrate this point:

It is not just interpreting. For instance, when they do the treadmill. The patient is walking. The interpreter is there constantly, saying, "Are you feeling okay? Any pain? Any discomfort? Any trouble breathing? You feel like you're going to faint?" The interpreter asks from one piece of paper that he gets: "How is the exercise now? Is it light? Regular? More difficult? Extremely difficult?" HCPs prefer interpreting face-to-face because they can see the facial expressions, the body language, if the patient is feeling uncomfortable, looks pale, sweaty, looks like [he] is going to pass out. But we interpreters are not doctors. We are not here to do that; we are there to interpret. But the truth is that the interpreter does not only play the role of interpreter; he plays multiple roles.

"That is a tremendous responsibility," I say to Roberto. He replies:

It is, it is, but it really helps the patient because the doctor is writing, looking at the graphic output. And he doesn't even look at the patient. And the interpreter is right there looking at the patient and asking, "How are you feeling?" The doctor does not keep eye contact with the patient and wants somebody else to do it. I mean, there is nothing wrong with it, if you can help in a way. But it's not the role of the interpreter either. Our role is limited. Our role is to interpret only.

Annette

Annette perceives the parties with whom she works as diverse, and she believes that working with them "can be as difficult or as easy as you make it, really." For her, the possibilities that interpreters have when they interact with patients or HCPs are numerous, and interpreters have choices in how they want to react when faced with challenges.

Annette sees patients as people who often do not have a high degree of education, but who are expressive and extremely trusting of those who take care of them. In her eyes, patients are often frightened too, because they are worried about their health.

As a non-native speaker of Spanish, she is aware of the different varieties of Spanish patients speak and does her best to make sure she is using terms and expressions they can understand. She adjusts her speech to the patients'. If unsure, she asks patients for help and lets them know that this task is difficult for her too, and that it is completely normal to ask others for help. In doing so, she creates a bond with patients, which results in a team effort to achieve effective communication.

For Annette the secret to success in communication is

to try and follow the lead of the patients at their level. And then . . . give [HCPs] some sort of idea of what level they're coming from, so that they can understand why the patient is expressing herself in that manner. Rather than, okay, cut-and-dry: the patient said this; doctor said that. Because neither one is going to get the essence of what is being said. Or at least, I don't think they'll get the essence, because they're coming from two different levels.

Annette is aware of the social differences that exist between the two parties for whom she works and tries to broker them by alerting the parties to those differences. She says this is the result of "what I would want said to me." So by putting herself in both parties' shoes, she tries to supply the needs that both may have. In this way, if the doctor has a cut-and-dry tone, she will soften it for the patient. She does a similar thing with the patient. In her words:

If the tone of the patient is on edge, I'll ask him to blow off steam with me first, so that we can then cut through all of that and get to the meat of the problem. It is not a comfortable situation for either party. You know [that something] is going [into] your body, but you don't know what it is. And you may not have the words to express it. And the other party is there to help you. But if they don't get the gist of what is happening, they can't [help].

It is evident that Annette plays a very proactive role in facilitating communication. She values the exchange that doctor and patient have so much that she will go the extra mile to smooth things out, in order for that exchange to be as productive for both parties as it can possibly be.

Annette believes she can do this because she connects well with people. Whenever she comes across obstacles, she works around them. When doctors use technical terms or complicated language, she breaks it down for patients to understand. Annette comments on the pain rating scale:

With a scale of one to ten, I basically just explain that what they would like to know is, one being no pain or . . . something you totally ignore, and ten being something worse than anything you've ever imagined. And we're talking about right now. Because I like to clarify that it isn't [about] what [the pain] was . . . but rather what is it now. So that we have an idea of what we're working with.

Triggered by her perceptions of the patient's understanding, Annette uses expanding, describing, explaining, and paraphrasing as some of the various strategies to enable comprehension (cf. Wadensjö 1998, 2000 classification of renditions). As she does this, she tries to bear in mind that patients are already under stress because they are dealing with health issues. Annette attempts to diminish that stress by avoiding the use of technical terms and by trying to break down any obstacles to communication. She knows that patients need to both understand their HCP (be informed) and feel comfortable, so that they can handle the health issue in the best possible way. Annette also realizes that the HCP must be able to trust the interpreter. If she expands on what the HCP has said, or she explains something to the patient, she is careful to keep the English speaker in the loop.

Annette values the trust of both parties in her work. If she summarizes a patient's story, she informs the doctor about the main points and lets him/her make the decision as to how much content she needs. Annette also does a lot of editing, because she considers this to be her responsibility. She can do this because of trust. But trust is not merely given to her; she works for it, actively seeking it. Annette feels that her tone of voice is instrumental in building trust. She explains:

I really don't have that problem with doctors . . . in as much as I . . . try to be a confiding voice for the patient. I try to use my voice in a manner with the physician or the therapist so that they understand that I'm conveying to them what was being said. And [I try] to keep it as smooth a transition from one side to the other as possible.

Nevertheless, there have been occasions where HCPs have challenged that trust. They have questioned her rendition as not having been exactly what patients had said. Annette remembers her response:

If you like, I can stop interpreting. I mean, my understanding wasn't that; it was this, although it sounds similar to such and such in our language. But if you . . . feel you might get a more accurate idea of what they're saying, I can log off, or step out or whatever is more convenient for you. I want you to be comfortable that you're getting the information you need.

Annette believes this to be an effective way of reminding the English speakers that if they really understand Spanish, then they should not need her in the first place. She politely exercises her power. She recalls instances where physicians have even apologized.

When sources of tension emerge with one of the parties in an ICE, Annette feels that it is equally simple or equally difficult to work with either of them. She does not feel more aligned with one party or the other. However, she recalls one situation where she crossed a boundary on the basis of her being a mother:

> For example, last week I was in the emergency room and a young man came in and his arm had [been] mangled in a cement mixer. Twenty-years old! A baby! I have a daughter older than him (pause) . . . so I was rubbing his eyebrow the whole time. Somebody said to me afterward that that could have been open to a terrible misinterpretation. But I just instinctively . . . comforted him as best I could, as a mother . . . rubbing the brow. But sometimes, I do tend to speak more . . . on a more familiar basis . . . with the patients, not disrespectfully.

Annette understands that she should be more cognizant and respectful of boundaries since crossing them could be a source of misinterpretation. Overall, Annette sees herself as a communicator, as a bridge that may exist built on the trust of those crossing it.

Consuelo

Consuelo sees her role as extremely varied. For her every ICE is unique, and so are the people for whom she works. Consuelo is keenly aware of class differences. She identifies people who have more formal education as easier to talk with and people with less education as more difficult. She tailors her word choices as much according to level of education as to regional varieties. She feels that she tailors her language much more towards patients' needs than to HCPs' needs. According to Consuelo, patients need simpler things, and she is happy to help them by simplifying complicated terms and medicalese. However, she does not embellish patients' talk when she communicates the message to the HCPs.

Consuelo perceives doctors as somewhat difficult to work with, since they are very "dry." Because doctors are abrupt in the way they sometimes talk to patients, Consuelo finds herself smoothing things for patients. She believes that understanding is better achieved if problems are ironed out. She says that sometimes patients unwillingly create obstacles in communication. When patients cannot stay focused or do not give an answer to a question, but rather tell a story, Consuelo limits their speaking time. She is always very polite but rigorous about keeping patients on track. She recalls an instance when this happened: "If it's . . . a fifteen-minute visit, . . . I say, . . . 'Unfortunately, we don't have much time for this. The doctor doesn't have much time for this. So we are only going to address the one problem. Is that okay?' And then . . . they understand."

Just as she disciplines patients, Consuelo also disciplines HCPs by altering their tone if necessary. She states:

Um. yesterday there was a patient here that had itching on the body and itching on the head. The doctor said, "Okay, I give you cream for the arms and cream for the head. Okay? So wait outside." But the patient said, "No, but I have a little sore in the vaginal area, and it's hurting a lot." The doctor said, "I can only give you for the arm . . . and for the head. So for that you're gonna have to call your doctor. So (mimicking abrupt tone of doctor) wait outside." I said to myself, "How do you improve this Consuelo?" because . . . I don't want to be as rude as the doctor. Sometimes he sounds very hard, like . . . um, I don't want to say rude . . . but sometimes . . . I don't know if it's the doctor's culture or what. And the patient felt rushed. I felt rushed. And yet, I was trying to smooth it a little.

In this way, Consuelo tones down the dryness or rudeness that she sometimes perceives on the part of rushed HCPs. It is interesting to note that Consuelo is very conscious of the pressure chain. She feels rushed or pressed by the HCP; therefore, she presses or rushes the patient. She sometimes perceives patients as rude and has to smooth them. She recalls an occasion when she politely introduced herself to the patient and asked him the reason for the visit by saying, "How can we help you? What's wrong with you?" And the patient replied, "If I knew what was wrong I would tell you, but I don't know what's wrong. If I wasn't sick, I wouldn't be here." Consuelo says that on that particular occasion, the doctor was the polite one. Although Consuelo believes that part of her role is to smooth things, when she defines her role she says, "I just interpret . . . I smooth things, but it's mainly interpreting and just opening up the communication."

Consuelo focuses on who patients are, where they come from, and what they bring to the encounter. She tries to achieve a social understanding of patients as a whole rather than to just pay attention to the linguistic variety they use. When she gains this understanding, she shares it with HCPs, among whom she finds variation in terms of patience and curiosity. Some doctors want to know everything, and others want only the information they requested. This is why Consuelo sometimes finds herself relaying a six-sentence answer into a four-word phrase. She gives the following example to illustrate this point:

I ask the patient, "Have you had a headache?" And the patient says, "Well, I had a headache . . . and my husband says that I shouldn't be complaining. But then I said, 'I do have a headache,' so I decided to come. And he said I don't have to come." So I [Consuelo] say to the doctor, "Well, she has a headache," and the doctor says, "She said more . . . than that." So I go on to tell him, "What she says [is that] she has a headache, but the husband says that she doesn't have one . . ." and the doctor quickly tells me, "Oh, okay, that's enough."

Consuelo shows that she has the power to decide what is relevant and what is not in order to answer a question, and she takes responsibility for that choice. The interpreter uses the power to cater to the HCPs' needs and not necessarily to the patients'. If the question is not answered, Consuelo believes it is up to the doctor to keep researching until she gets to the root of the problem really. Contrary to other interpreters who might feel a responsibility to bring the information to light, Consuelo thinks it is up to the parties to do that.

On many occasions, Consuelo feels emotionally trapped by either patients or HCPs. She prefers not to do too many interpreting jobs for the same parties (to avoid emotional attachment), but she is aware of patients' expectations (e.g. helping them out, holding their hands, or comforting them). She tries to detach herself emotionally from the parties, without seeming indifferent. She also senses expectations on the part of some HCPs who request her over any other interpreter. Although she tells HCPs any member of the interpreting team is equally professional, she believes that HCPs also become attached to certain interpreters and feel more comfortable working with someone they already know. But success does not depend only on the relationship between HCP and interpreters. Sometimes patients just do not want to hear bad news. She recalls one particular case where a doctor discussed resuscitation measures with a patient:

Patients don't want to hear *code blue*, and [sometimes] patients die. Of course, they might need CPR, but they don't . . . want to talk about it. And they said, "If you do that to me, that means I'm gonna die. And I don't wanna . . . don't talk to me." That is the hardest, to talk about codes. Of course everybody's gonna get scared. Everybody is scared about knowing that they [could] die.

When recalling other stressful moments, such as interpreting the pain rating scale, Consuelo states that she does not explain it to patients, because it is not her role. If the patient does not understand it, she conveys this to the HCP. Consuelo believes that her role is just to interpret.

Consuelo is aware of the complexity and variety of her role, which she defines as one of "non-alignment and just interpreting." She helps patients navigate the system by supporting them and leading them as she also opens their lines of communication with the other parties.

Elda

Elda says that the patients for whom she interprets come from Latin America: many from Mexico and Central America and a few from South America. When she thinks about similarities and differences among them, she first acknowledges cultural differences. She perceives doctors in America as being informal, because "they show up to appointments wearing tennis shoes." Elda feels that this is a shock to some Hispanic people, who are used to seeing the doctor as a figure of authority, so "some patients cannot believe that the person in front of them is, in fact, the doctor, [and they] keep asking me for the real one."

Elda reflects on the lack of education that some patients have and how she handles doctors' medicalese with them. She always starts high on the scale of politeness, and even uses euphemisms to refer to bodily functions; otherwise she may risk insulting the patient. She learned this from her brother who was a doctor in Mexico and worked with less privileged patients. She shared a story about the first time he had to ask a rural illiterate patient how many times a day he had a bowel movement. Her brother directly addressed the patient using the vulgar term for bodily function, that Elda considers low register: "*Y usted, ¿cuántas veces caga?*" (And, you, how many times do you shit?) Her brother's professor pulled him out of the room, told him that was unacceptable, and explained to him that he should always start with the most proper term when talking with a patient, and then go down the scale little by little, as needed. The opposite was not an option. One could not approach a patient with that kind of language, even if afterwards one realized that it was the only language the patient could understand.

Elda learned from her brother's experience. When speaking with patients, she always starts at the highest level. She uses the imagery of riding an elegant horse to describe her methodology: if necessary, she comes down from the horse, then she walks and if necessary, she crawls. She is willing to go as low as is necessary in order to communicate with the patient, but she never starts low. Interestingly, the way Elda refuses to start at the patient's level may lead one to believe that she perceives the patient's register as offensive or non-acceptable, evidently less elegant. Elda comments that patients insist on being heard and telling their stories: "Doctors are under time constraints, and most of the time they do not want to listen to those stories." Elda has seen the disappointment in some patients' faces when they are not heard. She also refers to "those patients who do not want to talk about their problems at all." She recalls a case when she was asking a patient his reason for coming to the hospital, and the patient was not answering. Elda had to pull information out of the patient as if she were using a corkscrew:

"*¿Qué es lo que tiene?*" (What is wrong?) "*Pos nada.*" (Nothing) "*Pero, ¿por qué vino a ver al doctor?*" (So why did you come to the doctor?) "*No sé.*" (I don't know.) So, one has to look for the information, as if you were a detective at times. I know that I am not only an interpreter. But here, it is more than interpreting, because at times you have to get information from the patient, almost like pulling teeth.

Elda, just like Annette, considers her tone of voice an essential tool for communication. She uses a soft tone to ask about the patients' symptoms. She knows that if patients perceive her as nice and helpful, they will be more cooperative than if they think she is harsh. Therefore, Elda sees her tone of voice as a door to patients' trust. She explains: "If you speak to a patient in a soft tone, the patient will pay attention to you. If you use an arrogant tone, not that you are arrogant, but you sound like it, patients don't like you, and they don't want you to interpret for them, but if you speak to them in a nice tone, you win patients' trust, you win them over."

It seems that patients and interpreters accomplish more in terms of communication when they form a partnership. The same holds true for interpreters and HCPs. True collaboration and partnership appear to be the keys to effective and efficient interaction. Elda is aware of this and makes it a priority in her work. In seeking collaboration, Elda balances differences. She believes that for the patient, it is essential to talk and create rapport. For the doctors it is essential to extract only the information they need and not to lose time with unnecessary details. Elda balances these differences by summarizing information for doctors and creating rapport with patients. In balancing styles and cultures, she never forgets to add a human touch. She believes that her passion for her work coupled with her human touch allows her to succeed, even in difficult circumstances. She will go the extra mile to comfort the patient and open up communication channels. She explains:

Many times I've had to go to the delivery room and have had to take the patient by the hand and help her, right? Then you say to yourself, "Well, here I am not doing only interpreting, I am helping her . . . in this moment." See, you help by giving patients a little confidence, by giving comfort. What . . . you are doing there, I don't know, but you know you have to do it.

For Elda, her role goes beyond switching languages. For her, being an interpreter means being a facilitator, an advocate, a pathway paver, and a true partner in communication.

Joaquín

Joaquín emphasizes the fact that CH is a teaching hospital. The HCPs with whom he works vary from interns to students to experienced doctors, to nurses and clerks. Spanish-speaking patients are mostly from Mexico and Central America, and they have little formal education. Contrary to other interpreters who may see patients' lack of education as an interpreting challenge, Joaquín believes that the biggest challenge caused by the low level of formal education is for doctors to understand how the patients explain their problems. Doctors are not always familiar with patients' background, sufferings, or fears. He says that patients have little formal education, which at times represents a challenge. It is necessary first to understand the symptoms and then to explain them to the doctor who, according to Joaquín "has no idea where patients [are] from, or [of] their habits, or . . . the social circumstances that caused them to develop the uneasiness that they feel or the illnesses."

For Joaquín, doctors vary in their reactions to these cultural differences. Some make an effort to understand the patients' ways of talking about their problems. Others want the problems to fit into their own schema, regardless of social circumstances and variation. In Joaquín's eyes, differences among doctors are more important than differences between languages and culture that are always present in a doctor–patient relationship. Joaquín notes that patients generally come to the clinic with a self-made diagnosis. Many times patients believe they are having the same problem as one of their relatives. Joaquín does not dismiss this information as useless or unsolicited. He looks for elements that might be helpful to the doctor's understanding of the patient.

For Joaquín, both patient and HCP represent the same challenge to effective communication. Patients are challenging because they cannot always describe a problem. HCPs are challenging because they are not always open to social differences that have not been addressed in their medical education. Alignment or identification with one of the parties is a fluid concept for Joaquín. Alignment depends upon the situation. However, one thing is stable: he identifies and aligns with whoever is necessary, in order to make understanding possible. He acknowledges that alignment is also linked to attitudes. He aligns with the party that is nicer to him or that does not have an attitude; with the one that is the weaker, in order to establish power balance, or with the one that needs more information in order to gain an understanding of the problem. In the last case, Joaquín takes it upon himself to offer a clarification. He says:

The truth is that you are flooded by attitudes here, more than you want to interpret. If a patient comes with an attitude towards you or towards the doctor, I believe that it is natural that you do more [to help] when there will be more . . . sympathy towards you. If it is a rude doctor that does not want to listen to the patient, then you have to take the side of the patient to be sure that the patient gets heard, that the patient asks the questions that she has to ask, and that the patient understands. Sometimes the doctor says to me, "Tell him not to do this," and he does not say why. Most of the patients are not going to follow instructions unless they understand the consequences of not following them. For example, if a mother comes with a baby and asks for cough syrup, and the doctor says, "No, tell them that we do not like giving cough syrup to the babies," I take it upon myself to explain that doctors do not like to give babies cough syrup, because they think that the cough helps to clean the baby's lungs and get rid of the phlegm, and if they give the baby [this] syrup, there is a risk of sediments accumulating. So, in five seconds I have explained the patient the reason and the patient does not feel that the doctor doesn't want to help.

Joaquín knows that doctors are always pressed for time. He also realizes that patients sometimes contribute to these pressures by telling long stories rather than answering questions. This tension between relevant and irrelevant information leads Joaquín to liken his role to picking through the trash for diamonds: *"Es como estar escogiendo los diamantitos en la basura, verdad, es importante lo que está diciendo el paciente, y es una decisión muy personal del intérprete y del doctor de querer oírlo."* (It is like looking for diamonds in the trash, right, what the patient is saying is important, and it is the interpreter's and the doctor's decision to want to hear it.)

Joaquín states that sometimes patients can be very irritating. Often they believe they can abuse the system, and treat everybody like their servants. According to Joaquín, this is the idea that some patients have of a public hospital. If the patients' expectations are not met, they argue with the interpreters, sometimes even expressing doubt as to the interpreters' willingness to help. When this happens, Joaquín uses a severe tone of voice and informs patients that if they do not like the system or if they have so many complaints, then they can consider their other options. But Joaquín does not react in the same way with doctors. Some doctors do not like to be corrected, and Joaquín is conscious of the hierarchy in place at CH. He demonstrates this as he says: *"Al doctor no lo puedes interrumpir aquí es muy serio ponerte a las patadas con los doctores* (laughter). *Por la jerarquía que hay, aquí el doctor es el Dios y de ahí para abajo todos."* (You can't interrupt a doctor here because it is very important that you don't lock horns with the doctors . . . due to the hierarchy . . . here, the doctor is God and everyone else is below him.) Joaquín observes that sometimes doctors do not explain enough to patients and patients are shy to ask more than once and, oftentimes, not even once. They are ashamed to acknowledge that they do not understand. So, they always answer "yes" to the question "do you understand?". Joaquín says that doctors, in turn, either give up trying to explain or inadvertently offend patients by asking them to repeat what they understood. Although he is aware of these differences, he sometimes feels that he lacks the power to explain them to doctors. He thinks he needs to gain the parties' trust, so challenging them is not a good option. Joaquín does not perceive all HCPs as being equally respectful or disrespectful towards patients. He perceives those with more seniority as more understanding, and less harsh than the younger ones. In brief, Joaquín explains his role as that of a filter, because he helps the two parties communicate by filtering out the obstacles that might prevent effective communication. In filtering, he also sees himself paving the way for better communication, since the filter does not allow insults or lack of respect to get through. When asked how he uses the filter, Joaquín says:

Le hago saber al médico de alguna manera que el paciente está molesto pero no creo que vaya a servir ningún propósito positivo, el decirle al doctor que cara de chin, pendejo, (risa) o igual donde los doctores no, hay doctores que son muy groseros, muy poquitos pero llega a haber, y si dicen algo ofensivo, o algo que va a hacer sentir mal al paciente no lo digo, y nunca ninguno me ha cuestionado eso, que no diga las groserías que dijeron o, o los desprecios, y yo entiendo que, a veces cuando uno dice algo, no está bien conectada la lengua con el cerebro y en ese momento cuando sienten mi silencio entienden que la cagaron. (I let the doctor know somehow that the patient is upset but I do not believe that it is going to serve any purpose to relay "idiot," or "dumbshit." It's the same with doctors. There are some doctors who are rude, few of them, but there are some, and if they say something offensive, or something that will upset the patient, I do not say it, and none of them have ever questioned me for this, that I do not say the vulgarity that was said, or express the disdain, and I think that sometimes when someone says something like that, there is a misconnection between the tongue and the brain, and it is then, when they can feel my silence, that they understand they messed up.)

Filtering out or selecting information is a tremendous responsibility that Joaquín places upon himself, especially because he is aware of all the beliefs and prejudices that he possesses which may color the decisions he makes. In his words: *"Es mucha responsabilidad, mucha responsabilidad, porque tú como intérprete eres una persona con tus vicios, inclinaciones, tus complejos, tus creencias estúpidas que toda la gente la tiene, entonces es una responsabilidad muy grande porque tú decides qué se va a oír de este paciente."* (It is a big responsibility, a big responsibility, because as an interpreter, you are a person with your biases, inclinations, your complexes, your stupid beliefs that all people have, so it is a big responsibility because you decide what will be heard about this patient.) He adds that this ability to select is crucial to the job of medical interpreters, although many of his colleagues would not admit it:

Muy poca gente, creo, va a reconocer que hacen lo que yo te digo que hago, que es escoger desde la información lo que es mas útil, porque si no lo haces, corres el riesgo de que al doctor se le acabe el tiempo y el paciente no llega a lo que verdaderamente lo trajo a la clínica, entonces, esa es mucha responsabilidad, cada minuto que pasa, tienes tú la responsabilidad, o sea la oportunidad de corregirte, de traer esto que te dijeron allá atrás, que te quedaste callado y ponerlo aquí otra vez. Por ejemplo, muchas veces pasa esto, que el doctor le pregunta al paciente sobre un síntoma específico y él te platica de una parte, de otra parte del cuerpo, entonces tú lo guardas . . . y le recuerdas al paciente que a él le preguntaron de la rodilla no la oreja, al rato cuando el doctor ya subió para acá, entonces le dices al doctor, me dijo más al ratito que tenía esto en la oreja. (Very few people, I believe, are going to recognize that they do what I tell you I do. I choose from the information what is most useful because if you do not do this, you run the risk that the doctor will run out of time and the patient will not get to the issue that brought him to the clinic. So it is a big responsibility. Every minute that goes by you are responsible for, I mean you have the opportunity to correct yourself, to bring forward something that was told to you before and you did not convey. For example, many times the doctor asks the patient about a specific symptom and the patient talks about a different part of the body, so you keep that to yourself and you remind the patient that the doctor is asking about his knee not his ear. Then when the doctor gets up, then you say to him "the patient said before that he had this pain in his ear.")

Joaquín sees the need to select out information because of the time constraints of doctor–patient interviews. He fears that the doctor will leave the room and the patient will miss the occasion to communicate what was essential for the interview to be successful. Based on this fear, Joaquín places what he considers to be efficiency over neutrality. He does not believe that an interpreter can be efficient if he is worried about neutrality and transparency. He also notes how sometimes this alignment occurs on the basis of class (or other beliefs or prejudices) rather than on the basis of the communicative needs of the situation. He remarks: *"Noto aquí quizá porque los intérpretes con los que trabajo vienen de clase media, que hay la tendencia a alinearse con el doctor, a considerar al paciente como el que tiene información equivocada, como que es el ignorante, el único que se puede equivocar, y eso no está bien."* (I see that in here, maybe because the interpreters with whom I work are middle class, there is a tendency for interpreters to align with the doctor, to believe that the patient has the wrong piece of information, that the patient is the ignorant, that he is the only one who can make a mistake and that is not right.)

Joaquín bases his opinions about his colleagues' alignment with the doctor on his own observations. It is not that colleagues do or say anything openly about the patients; the institution would not tolerate that. Joaquín says that it is demonstrated in that extra mile that he feels they would not go for the patient, or sometimes in the additional comments they make to emphasize the doctor's remarks. For Joaquín, going the extra mile for a patient means making sure that he/she understands the information and can provide informed answers.

Julio

Julio sees his role as that of a bridge between cultures and languages; he makes patients and HCPs more accessible to one another. He sees the two parties for whom he interprets as being very different. In his eyes, HCPs are almost always pressed for time. However, patients usually have plenty of time and want to be heard. HCPs relate to patients to discover facts that will help them make a diagnosis. Patients, on the other hand, answer HCPs' questions but they also want attention and look to HCPs for rapport as well as for report. These opposite interests sometimes frustrate Julio, and he desperately tries to bring HCP and patient closer together. In doing so, he exercises his power to keep the patient focused. He does this by repeating the question and reminding the patient that he/she simply needs to answer it. In this way he tries to avoid story telling or what he considers unnecessary information that may result in loss of time for all parties involved. Julio also helps HCPs by simplifying what he refers to as *palabras de domingo* (fancy words) and making the medical jargon more accessible to patients.

But HCPs are not the only ones who use medical terms. Sometimes Julio asks for symptoms and patients respond with a self-diagnosis. For example he recalls asking a patient, *"¿Qué le duele?"* (What hurts?), and the patient responds,

"Tengo infección de los pulmones" (I have a lung infection). Julio then re-directs the patient to the symptoms (and away from the self-diagnosis), so that the symptoms can be explored during the visit. He does this by asking more general questions. Sometimes he needs to ask several questions since patients' self-diagnoses are not always evident to him. For Julio, one of the biggest challenges is the affective role that is sometimes imposed on the interpreter. He gets to know some of the patients really well. Patients rely on him not only to communicate but also for moral support and sometimes even personal advice. Julio believes that this is because patients identify more with him than with the HCPs on the basis of culture.

In some cases, this identification based on cultural commonalities is also encouraged by HCPs' behaviors. To illustrate this, Julio recalls a pediatrics case in which he interpreted for the patient and the resident doctor in front of the senior doctor. The patient was a ten-year-old boy with a bedwetting problem who was accompanied by his parents. When the resident presented his case and his diagnosis to the attending physician, the senior doctor turned to Julio and asked what he thought about the case. Julio recalls feeling uncomfortable in that situation, because he is not a doctor, but mostly because the resident was present. The attending physician explained that he noticed how Julio was watching the interaction between the boy and his parents, while the resident doctor was busy taking notes to prepare the medical history. The senior doctor also said that the interaction was probably typical of a Hispanic parent and child, and that was the reason why he wanted to know Julio's opinion, since interpreters routinely focus on cultural issues. Julio told the attending physician, "I noticed that father and child did not talk to each other. The mother seems to be very protective. She is now pregnant and she mentioned that she is married to a new husband that does not get along really well with the child." Julio feels that his duties extend beyond that of language switching. As an interpreter, he is actively engaged in obtaining what he thinks is necessary information. He is also aware of the cross-culturally acceptable way of delivering information to patients. He believes this is one of the areas where HCPs rely heavily on interpreters' expertise.

He recalls a situation when a patient coming from Mexico to seek treatment in the US died on the airplane en route to the US. The patient was accompanied by five female family members. Julio attempts to explain the economic burden that the trip had put on this humble family. The family was hoping that the hospital could cure the patient. All their faith (and life savings) had been invested in the surgical intervention that the patient was supposed to undergo. When the family members received the news that the man had died on the flight, the five women began to scream and cry. Julio was abashed at the abruptness with which the news had been broken. He wished that he had been asked for his advice in how to deliver the bad news. He says that Hispanic patients are not used to receiving such news in a harsh, direct manner; they believe that bad news should sometimes be watered down. For Julio, being an interpreter is like being a cultural and language bridge that brings parties closer to one another.

Marcos

Marcos perceives the patients at CH as quite uniform. He describes the average patient for whom he interprets as a lower-working-class immigrant, for the most part from Mexico but also from Central America, and with a low educational level and with "all the characteristics of Hispanic people." Those characteristics for Marcos include non-compliance with medicine instructions, especially if they are feeling better, and fear of asking questions. According to Marcos, patients are afraid to ask for clarification or repetition. Marcos has learned to gauge whether or not patients understand the explanations given to them, by their tone of voice. He then follows his instincts, and repeats the information to the patients, as many times as he feels are necessary.

Marcos blames the patients' difficulty in understanding what they are told in Spanish on their lack of education. He also finds it more difficult to communicate with patients than with HCPs. Interestingly, Marcos is the only interpreter who perceives HCPs as being sensitive to patients' registers and flexible in adapting their language to the patients' level. Marcos is reluctant to admit that he helps patients understand the HCPs' words. He believes he is neutral and he only interprets. Marcos communicates easily with HCPs, although he acknowledges that sometimes they use unnecessarily difficult terms. When I asked Marcos about the pain scale, he says that it is impossible to assign numbers to pain and patients do not know how to quantify pain. In his experience, nurses impose the scale more than doctors do. He also mentions that when patients tell stories instead of answering the questions, he follows the doctors' lead. He corners the patients until he gets the answers that the HCPs need. He believes that it is part of his role. However, he does not discard the patients' stories. He saves them until after the crucial questions have been answered.

An important facet of Marcos' role is to prioritize information and present it at the right time. He feels a big sense of responsibility to filter the right information at the right moment, but the parameter he uses to measure relevant information is based on the HCP's availability. He does not want to make doctors lose time. If certain comments are not worthy of the doctor's attention, he simply eliminates them: *"Tú sabes más o menos cuando el paciente está hablando tonterías, que no vienen al caso. Entonces esas ni vale la pena mencionárselas al doctor."* (You know more or less when the patient is saying silly things that are not to the point. Then they are not worth mentioning to the doctor.)

Unlike Consuelo, Marcos does not perceive the HCPs as being abrupt or dry, so he never feels the need to smooth their words. But he does so for nurses whom he perceives to behave harshly toward patients. Marcos is always ready to soften their words and avoid the feeling of shame that those words may cause to patients. He explains: *"Las enfermeras a veces tratan de regañar al paciente por algo. Entonces no – uno conoce a su gente, no se le habla mal al paciente porque se molesta. Uno se molesta con facilidad."* (Nurses at times try to reprimand a patient for something. So, no – one knows one's people; you don't speak badly to the patient because he will be upset. One gets upset easily.)

Even if Marcos perceives himself as neutral, the fact that he protects the patients from uncomfortable situations is evidence of how he aligns with parties. His words *"uno conoce a su gente"* (one knows one's people) are a reflection of this. He works to protect patients from feeling uncomfortable, and from patronizing or harsh attitudes on the part of nurses.

The protection that Marcos offers is not unconditional, however. When a doctor has some bad news and tells it to the patient directly, Marcos does not water it down for the patient. If the doctor is abrupt, Marcos is also abrupt. When Marcos reflects on his role, he believes that it is to make people understand each other. He acknowledges the fact that this is not a simple task. He continues to believe that patients are responsible for making this understanding happen. He recalls the case of a patient to whom he had to repeat the dosage of a medicine numerous times. He was not sure the patient was following him. He asked the patient to write it down and repeat it in loud voice and the patient was still making mistakes. Finally Marcos realized that the patient was illiterate.

Mariana

Mariana believes she is the *"lazo de unión entre el paciente y el doctor"* (the bond between the patient and the doctor). She is keenly aware of power differentials between the parties for whom she interprets. She sees doctors, nurses, technicians, and staff as members of the same team as interpreters, and the goal of that team is to provide patients with the best healthcare possible. For Mariana HCPs have the knowledge and the power to make a diagnosis, to order treatment and to educate patients. When they use technical terms, she explains those to the patient. She would not, however, use a less technical term (uttered by the patient) when she addresses the HCP. She explains: *"Igualmente cuando el paciente viene y se queja que le duele la panza, tú no le vas a decir al doctor que le está doliendo la panza o el pescuezo, verdad. Uno tiene que decir el cuello o el estómago."* (Similarly when the patient comes and he is complaining that his belly hurts, you are not going to tell the doctor that the belly or neck is hurting, right? One has to say neck or stomach.)

Part of her job is to learn regionalisms that patients use. She does this by asking the patients to explain to her a little more whenever they use a term she does not know. She recalls: *"la primera vez que me dijeron 'tengo grima,' pensé qué será eso, entonces 'a ver explíqueme un poquito más, señor, porque no le*

entiendo bien.' 'Sí, la grima, la gana de vomitar.' 'Ah' dije, entonces ahora yo sé si alguien me dice que tiene grima yo sé que es que tiene nausea o asco."
(The first time they told me "I have *grima*," I thought what could this be, then I would say, "let's see – explain this to me a little more, sir, because I don't understand you well." "Yes, the *grima*, it makes you want to vomit." "Aha," I said. Now I know if someone tells me that they have *grima*, I know that they are nauseated or feel like gagging.)

Mariana thinks of her job as a life-learning one. Whenever she comes across terms she does not know she writes them down and keeps a running glossary. She also knows that, sometimes, brokering a term with a patient may require longer explanations and more time than the HCP may anticipate. She tells HCPs that she needs to explore more and that it may take her a little longer to interpret. According to Mariana, most of the doctors do not have a problem with this because they trust her. HCPs trust the seniority and experience that interpreters have. For Mariana it is easier to work with HCPs than with patients. She perceives doctors as very human. They respect patients and they are aware of patients' needs and limitations and they treat them nicely. She says that patients, on the other hand, can sometimes be very rude. When they have waited a long time, or if they do not get the prescription they think they need, they get very upset and can be rude. Many times they listen to family members' advice, and by the time they see the doctor, they have already decided which treatment they need. If the doctor's opinion is different, the patients become upset. Mariana believes that doctors take their time to educate patients about the options they have. In this educational process, doctors are neither patronizing nor lecturing the patients. They are always looking out for the patient's best interest, even if the patient sometimes finds this hard to believe. She feels that doctors always strive to be precise and accurate.

Mariana believes that this strife for accuracy might be triggered by the fear of being sued. She compares the Mexican and American perceptions of medicine. She is familiar with the Mexican perspective, not only because she is Mexican, but also because her husband is a physician in Mexico. She claims familiarity with the Mexican medical culture where, in her opinion, doctors are not under a constant threat of legal action as they are in the US. She says, "Mexican physicians are treated with respect. They enjoy trust." Mariana says that doctors do not need to resort to the precision of scales in Mexico to rate pain, but they describe pain as *"leve, moderado o severo"* (light, medium or severe). When she hears doctors using the pain scale, Mariana sometimes tries to explain to them that patients think differently about pain and that they might need more explanation. Some doctors are very receptive of her feedback. For Mariana being an interpreter is like being a team player in a very complex game. She sees the role as multifaceted. It is a combination of adapting cultures and making concepts relevant and understandable so that both parties can communicate.

Mauro

Mauro believes that he is the patient's voice; he says that the patient justifies his job. He is aware of the differences in educational level between the parties for whom he interprets. Since he is committed to facilitating communication, he will align with any of the parties during an ICE, as long as it will help him achieve what he considers a successful doctor–patient interview. Mauro reflects on how he can explain to the patient the importance of answering questions or of delivering the necessary information that an HCP may need, in order to best serve him/her. He believes that sometimes patients fail to see the importance of staying focused and understanding what is being discussed. He recalls: *"Muchas veces se traen dos o tres chiquitines a la consulta, están corriendo y a todo dicen que sí. El médico les está explicando algo, ellos dicen que sí, pero más atención le están prestando al chiquitín que se está subiendo a la mesa."* (Often they bring two or three children to the appointment, who keep running around. They say yes to everything. The doctor is explaining something to them, they say yes, but they are paying more attention to the child who is climbing on the table.)

Mauro's viewpoint on his role is that it varies from one ICE to another. Sometimes he must be patient, and other times he feels the need to be harsh, especially when patients do not pay attention. He perceives himself as an arbitrator, having to mediate between both parties and deciding when he is going to tone down harsh comments, or when he will harden words that are a little too soft. He emphasizes that he needs to be extremely sensitive to the patient's tone, intonation, volume, and insulting comments. He has learned how to tell how a patient is feeling and how much information the patient is accessing by listening to the tone of voice. Mauro compares the information obtained through body language when doing face-to-face interpreting with the information obtained by the tone of voice when interpreting over the speakerphone. He acknowledges that patients are often focused only on the interpreters. Sometimes patients not only speak directly to him, but they also call him doctor.

For Mauro it is easier to interact with patients than with HCPs, because he shares the same linguistic and cultural background with the former. He also sees his role as much more relevant for patients than for HCPs. He perceives patients as extremely distinct, whereas doctors are more uniform. He says that he "glosses" concepts to make them more accessible to patients. One example is the pain scale. Oftentimes, Mauro finds himself suggesting different ways of saying the same thing to doctors. He recalls saying, *"Qué le parece si le preguntamos si el dolor es ligero, moderado, o severo, si quiere usted un poquito, más, más exacto es de ligero a moderado, o de moderado a severo y si es típicamente moderado, o si es típicamente severo, y punto ¿verdad?"* (What if we ask the patient if the pain is light, moderate, or severe, or, if he [the doctor] wants to be a little more precise, I can say light to moderate, moderate to severe and if it is typically moderate or if it is typically severe. Right?)

When Mauro reflects on his role, he realizes that his alignment with each party varies according to the nature of the situation. In an emergency situation, if the patient does not answer the questions, Mauro tries to focus him/her on answering the questions accurately. In other words, he aligns with the information much more than with the parties. He sees his job as a link between patient and HCP, to help the parties communicate with no loss of information. He considers himself a door opener, or someone who helps patients navigate the system. He goes the extra mile for patients, and he does this out of good will. He describes his role as that of a bilingual social worker. His willingness to help is not biased towards one party only. He is there to assist all parties to the ICE equally, and he is committed to serving the hospital community with his work.

Rogelio

Rogelio likens his position as interpreter to standing on the edge of a sea cliff. He perceives his role as complex, very complicated. He feels the need to maintain a balance between patients who are used to being heard and who need to express themselves, and doctors who get impatient when time is lost in building rapport. While keeping that balance, Rogelio must maintain objectivity. If he spends too much time talking to patients, he says that HCPs sometimes suspect that he is giving advice, or they wonder what he could be saying that is taking him so long. Usually, what Rogelio is trying to do in those instances is pass information along, but in a more understandable way, in an attempt to build *"un colchón de confianza."* By listening to a patient's voice or watching his/her body language, Rogelio monitors the patient's trust towards him. He says that in general, patients at CH are very kind, and more often than not, they believe that doctors are the Almighty. They do not question what they are told unless they do not like the HCP. If they cannot trust the HCP, they will probably not comply.

Rogelio perceives a big gap between the parties for whom he interprets. He thinks that the difference in education between HCPs and patients is notorious, but not all patients are similar. Some (generally political refugees) challenge and question the doctor's opinion. They inquire about the details of treatment and how decisions were made; they request second opinions. They use medicalese as doctors do. Rogelio sees no need to explain any sophisticated term to them. On the other hand, when patients do not have what he perceives as enough education, Rogelio brokers terms for them and tones down some of their comments, as they can be offensive to the HCPs. For example, he mentions how patients complain when they have spent too much time waiting or when they are expected to have answers to health questions that HCPs ask.

He believes that patients often do not see the importance of attending classes or complying with preventive medicine. Sometimes they do not follow instructions on a treatment or a diet because either they do not understand the value, or because scientific instructions contradict their folk beliefs. Rogelio recalls when patients admit they have not been taking the medicine for cholesterol because *"la comadre Juana me dio jugo de nopal y con eso se me quita."* (*Comadre Juana* gave me nopal juice and it goes away with that.) Rogelio blames the patients' non-compliance on the medical system of their country of origin. As a doctor himself in Mexico, Rogelio has seen patients, for example, go to the doctor when they are sick, rather than when they want to stay healthy. In his mind, patients do not understand the preventive aspects of American medicine. He thinks the American system fails to communicate the value of preventive medicine to patients coming from other countries. In this system, doctors are always pressed for time; patients feel that the doctors are not interested in them as people. So, they do not trust in the care they receive, and they do not follow instructions. In Mexico where Rogelio studied medicine, he was constantly reminded that he was not treating the illness he was treating the ill person.

As an interpreter, Rogelio feels a need to help patients understand the value of compliance. Even if it takes longer, he reassures patients that he, and everyone else involved in the medical encounter, is there to help them get better. In his opinion, things such as pain scales and medical terms need to be brokered so that the patients can relate to them.

Rogelio is committed to helping patients, but he is also aware of the limitations imposed upon him (and on the type of service that he can render) by the system. When he is in his cubicle in front of his phone, he feels pressured by the red light. He knows that there are over five calls waiting. He tries to manage each call in the quickest and most effective manner possible. He feels that when doctors rush him, he has to rush patients even if he does not want to.

Vicente

Vicente likens his role to that of a mine digger. He is always digging to get to the hidden and valuable information. Sometimes, he must dig deeply in order to obtain it. He perceives the two parties for whom he works as very diverse. HCPs use difficult terms when they speak, and often his role is to simplify the message so patients can understand it. Patients have a modest education, and because HCPs assume that patients understand everything that is said, part of the interpreter's job is to educate HCPs in how to talk with patients. HCPs also make assumptions about patients' SES, for example when they ask patients if they can drive. (Most of the CH patients ride the bus or a bike.) Vicente also recognizes his role as an aid to HCPs, helping them to understand the patients' expectations and reactions, which are often triggered by their cultural background. Vicente remembers one occasion when he had to help an HCP deliver bad news in a culturally appropriate manner. Vicente has interpreted in delicate situations, such as the request for organ donations to the family of a patient who had just died:

> Some doctors are better at doing this than others. When I see, for example, that the doctor is not a person that will go into considering the family . . . or is pressed by time, as we all are, I take it upon myself to say "now the child is dead, and nothing can be done," and I continue to ask the family to think if the medicine of today could have another way to deal with the problem of which that person died, if they have some knowledge of some medicine to prevent that person from dying, trying to find out more about that disease. Or trying to prevent the person from dying by changing some of the parts of the body. And so little by little, one gets to the organs.

He recalls another situation in which the doctor in the emergency room needed a yes or no answer to the question: "Is he hypertensive?" The patient started telling a story from twenty years ago, and two sentences into the story the doctor told Vicente, "Tell him that I do not need to hear that crap." Vicente recalls not translating that statement, as it would not have helped the situation. Rather, he continued to elicit the yes or no answer and finally got it. Vicente emphasizes that part of his role is to educate both parties. He tells HCPs how to make culturally appropriate adjustments; he paves the way to questions that can otherwise be misinterpreted, and as he does this, he reminds HCPs that this process generally takes more time than communication with monolingual patients. Also, he educates patients in staying focused and complying with the HCPs' instructions.

For Vicente, it is easier to communicate with patients, but he also acknowledges that HCPs are "improving in dealing with cross-cultural patients, and patients in general." He thinks that this improvement may be due to the change in medical school programs in the last fifteen years. He thinks that doctors are less arrogant and proud than in the past. He believes that doctors in the US are pressed for time and are always on the watch for threats to their reputation (lawsuits). He recalls being perceived in the Hispanic culture with respect: "In the Hispanic culture, going to the doctor is like going to the priest."

As a doctor, Vicente is very critical of the technical terminology used in the hospital to communicate with patients. One example is the pain scale. In his opinion, defining pain can be very difficult for the patients, so scales need to be brokered, and examples should be given without suggesting answers. In brief, Vicente sees his role as that of an enabler of communication between two parties, allowing the doctor to understand the problem of the patient and vice versa. He sees himself as the "clarifier" of dark information.

Vicente is one of three interpreters who also happen to be foreign-trained physicians. The fact that so much variability exists between the interpreters' educational backgrounds raises several questions: what, if any, relationship exists between the interpreters' level of education and how they perceive their role during the medical encounter? Does a foreign-trained physician working as an interpreter take more ownership and orchestrate, expand, or summarize more, because of his prior knowledge of medicine? Is an interpreter with a high school education less likely to claim ownership of a text and explore answers to a line of medical interrogation, because he feels as though he has an inferior understanding of the line of questioning? In a study of interpreters' perceptions of their role discussed elsewhere (Angelelli 2003), level of education was not found to have a statistically significant relationship with interpreters' perceptions of visibility. And when we revisit the segments analyzed in chapter 6, it appears that the answer to all of these questions is no. The three interpreters whose education ends at the high school level were just as likely to create text as those who had Bachelor's, Master's, or Medical Degrees. Joaquín (high school) and Mariana (MA) both seem to take on the role of helper. Joaquín tries to make the pain scale numbers more concrete for the patient, narrowing the patient's options, and finally practically choosing a number for the patient. He is aware that he serves as a cultural broker and feels like this responsibility is part of his job. His expanded renditions are triggered by social factors. Julio (high school) takes ownership of text by pausing until he receives a patient's acknowledgment of understanding before proceeding. He takes initiative in telling a patient's parent not to give the child candy or gum before surgery, and he asks about loose teeth (chapter 6 segment 9). He admits to being a comprehension broker for the patient by simplifying or exemplifying when doctors use words that he thinks the patient will not understand. Both Consuelo (high school) and Marcos (BS) open and close encounters with patients using the norms of the patient's own culture. Annette (AS), Vicente (MD), and Rogelio (MD) all appear to perceive differences in levels of education among patients, and so they tailor their speech to that of the patient, sliding messages down the register scale, and they try to teach the patients (e.g. to write down appointments).

   In this chapter I have examined the role of the interpreter as discussed by the ten informants and the manager. These discussions were in the form of semi-structured interviews, in which interpreters reflected on the parties for whom they work, how they handle stressful situations, and their perceptions of their role. Through their words we can see how the impressions (Brewer 1988 in chapter 3) they form of others (HCPs and patients) trigger their behaviors during the ICEs. Some of the interpreters (e.g. Mariana) find patients to be problematic, because they lack the sophistication to understand what they are told. This perception of patients causes interpreters to feel responsible for brokering comprehension. For other interpreters (e.g. Joaquín), the HCPs are problematic, because they are unaware of the social reality of patients. While discussing stressful situations, such as the interpreting of the pain scale or a request for organ donation, interpreters agree that patients and HCPs differ (sometimes greatly) in their concepts of the reality with which they are working. Patients do not measure pain in the same way as providers, and sad news needs to be watered down for some patients. Interpreters' perceptions of patients, coupled with their assumptions and their social baggage (Bourdieu 1977 in chapter 3), play an important role in how they construct meaning. This echoes Duranti's conceptualization (1992) of the speaker's responsibility in constructing talk – a responsibility that is both contextually and cooperatively defined. As we have seen from these interviews, meaning should not be conceived as being owned by one of the individuals, but rather achieved cooperatively in the ICE. The combination of all the informants helped me gain a richer perspective on the cross-cultural communication they broker and on the tension between roles that unfolds in practice, and what they identify as the role expected of them. These reflections on their role, triangulated with the observations of these interpreters at work and what they wrote about their behaviors and beliefs in the IPRI, allow me to close the circle I opened to study the question of the interpreter's role.

8   Emerging metaphors and final words

In the ICEs they facilitate, interpreters play a wide variety of roles. In the present study, that variety was evidenced by how interpreters perceived their roles, enacted them, and talked about them. During interviews and conversations, the terms used by interpreters to talk about their roles illustrated the tension between the prescribed role (invisible) and the actual role (visible). However, this tension only seems to exist at the level of the perception or belief, because in practice, the tension gets resolved. The interpreters shadowed in this study became visible partners in their interpreted communicative events. Many of them described their varied roles using metaphors. In the following sections, we explore some of those metaphors.

Interpreters as detectives

As we saw in chapter 6, patients do not always give specific answers to HCPs' questions. Sometimes HCPs even ask interpreters to get information without giving them a specific script. Interpreters then take the lead in a line of questioning, in order to get the answer. In other words, they become detectives, questioning the patient carefully, hoping to discover the answer. Interpreters perceive this as an enormous responsibility, not just because the HCP depends on this answer to take action, but also because in many instances, interpreters have no guidance as to what exactly they are supposed to ask. In spite of this, interpreters willingly take on this responsibility.

This phenomenon is illustrated in chapter 6, segment 13, in which the patient on the phone is reporting symptoms of a heart attack to the nurse. The nurse does not speak Spanish, so she asks Mauro to find out if there is anyone else in the house. Mauro discovers that the only other person in the house (the landlady) speaks only Spanish. The nurse laughs helplessly as Mauro takes on the role of detective by first asking the patient questions, then convincing the patient to put the landlady on the line, and finally asking the landlady a series of questions about the patient's condition. Once he has received the information he needs, Mauro solves the case by convincing the landlady to call 911. All of this is done without the nurse's participation.

Although the level of most interpreters' formal education does not match that of the HCPs for whom they interpret, the interpreters still take on the role of detective when necessary. Using their own past experiences as a guide, they seldom stop to consider the tremendous responsibility or risk involved in taking this initiative. Like all good detectives, their main objective is to solve the case.

Interpreters as multi-purpose bridges

Interpreters are an essential part of the cross-cultural medical encounter. They occupy the unique position of understanding both interlocutors' points of view and points of reference. Although HCPs are equipped with the knowledge to provide a service to the patient, they can only apply that knowledge if they have information about the history of the patient's illness. Sometimes, this information can only be obtained with the help of an interpreter. Patients, on the other hand, have the answers that make HCPs' knowledge complete and applicable, but in order to access that care and knowledge, they must rely on an interpreter. Therefore, interpreters help each party gain access to the other's valuable information by relaying the message in a cross-linguistically and cross-culturally accessible format; they are listeners and speakers for both patients and HCPs.

Healthcare providers in today's American society often seem to be pressed for time. For many of them, history-taking and physical examination of the patient are intimately tied to relevance and efficiency but not necessarily to rapport. A patient's story is often irrelevant to his/her current illness. The HCP can usually afford to spend only enough time listening to obtain the information that is relevant to the matter at hand. However when trust is first established, this exploration is easier. Interpreters are usually willing to take the time to listen to the patient's story. Through their ability to navigate the cultural perspectives of both patients and providers, interpreters bridge these perspectives. They provide a service to both patients and HCPs, sometimes by educating the parties on cultural differences and other times by simply ironing out the differences without making either party aware of the process.

Recall in chapter 6, segment 7, when the doctor asked Elda to find out if the medicine had helped the patient. The patient began to tell a story, so Elda interrupted and then re-focused the patient on the question. Elda had been concerned that time would run out without the patient receiving the care she needed, because she had not supplied the necessary information. As evidenced by this example, the interpreter may interrupt in order to keep a patient focused on the relevant question, or alternatively, the interpreter may summarize and edit directly without explaining his/her strategy to either of the parties. When interpreters do this, they consider themselves to be bridges for the different levels of the cross-linguistic and cross-cultural encounter.

Interpreters as diamond connoisseurs

Patients' stories vary in terms of their content. Since these stories usually consist of a mixture of relevant, less relevant, or irrelevant pieces of information, the interpreter has to know how to discern the relevant pieces from the irrelevant ones. In the telling of a story, the patient opens up a bag full of rocks, diamonds, and dirt. In this metaphor, the diamonds represent the crucial elements of information that are needed for the interview to succeed, the rocks represent the irrelevant information, and the dirt is the discourse that glues them together.

It is important that interpreters be capable of distinguishing diamonds from ordinary rocks. This involves knowing how to look beyond appearances, since some rocks may look like ordinary rocks but in reality (under the dirt) are diamonds. What might seem like dirt or an ordinary rock at one point of the communicative event may become an extremely useful piece of information (a diamond) as the ICE unfolds. Distinguishing a diamond from an ordinary rock is no trivial job if both are covered with dirt; it represents an enormous responsibility for the interpreter.

The following example illustrates this. In one ICE, the patient's chief complaint was headache. The doctor wanted to know how long the patient had had that headache, so Joaquín asked. The patient immediately launched into a story about an automobile accident that he had had four years ago, thinking that the present headache was related to that accident. While this information could be useful, Joaquín knew that the doctor probably did not want to hear the whole story about the car accident. All he wanted to know was the duration of symptoms of this present illness. Joaquín saw the story of the accident as a stone that had potential of becoming a diamond, so he decided to keep the details of the story to himself (as just an ordinary stone) for the time being.

Interpreters as miners

While many patients like to tell stories, others are less willing to make the information readily available for interpreters or HCPs. In these cases, it is not enough for interpreters to know the linguistic and culturally acceptable way in which they can address a party to request information. Interpreters must find a way to extract the information. In this sense, interpreters are like miners. They excavate until they get to the gold (the necessary information).

Both recognizing that the gold is out there and going after it require a special skill. Interpreters are often faced with patients who are less than cooperative. Many patients feel pressured when they are asked a bunch of questions. They may lack understanding of the history-taking process, or they may simply be ashamed to admit that they do not know the answers to the questions being asked. Part of being an interpreter is in knowing how to ask the same question in several different ways. Interpreters must get beyond the vague answers by being gently persistent until they find the gold. This is illustrated in chapter 6, segment 11, in which a nurse asks Vicente to ask the patient "about chronic illnesses, diabetes . . . [and] all that." Vicente enters into a lengthy discussion with the patient about her entire medical history.

Vicente recognizes the need for the expertise of a miner in this case, so he generates specific questions and digs for answers until the patient opens the pathway to the gold. When he feels that he has struck it rich, he relays the information to the nurse.

Pulling it all together

In this book I have presented interpreters facilitating interpreted communicative events in a medical setting and examined the role of the interpreter during cross-cultural and cross-linguistic communication as an object of scholarly inquiry. The paradigm shift in the conceptualization of the role of the interpreter (from an invisible mechanical language expert to a visible co-participant with agency in the interaction) is echoed in the medical literature that addresses issues in healthcare access for speakers of non-societal languages. Both fields (medicine and interpreting studies) have called for a need to address those issues and have raised questions aiming to improve cross-cultural communication in a medical setting. Using an interdisciplinary lens from social theory, social psychology, and linguistic anthropology, I studied the role of interpreters by asking a question that I felt could be better answered using an ethnographic approach: what is the role of the hospital interpreter?

The research presented demonstrated that interpreters who are capable of highly complex information-processing tasks are also social human beings who facilitate cross-linguistic and cross-cultural communication. As such, they are engaged in the co-construction of meaning with other interlocutors within an institution, which is permeable to cultural norms and societal blueprints. Through the use of a variety of data sources and multiple analyses, this research traced the interpreters' role from the way they perceived themselves to the way they behaved when they were exercising their role, and even to the way they spoke about it.

In this study, interpreter's visibility impacted on the interaction at various levels. Sometimes this impact was highly consequential for the relay of medical or personal information. Sometimes it was not. Interpreters became visible by replacing one of the interlocutors, by aligning with the parties to channel information, by communicating affect, by exploring, by expanding or summarizing triggered by social factors, and by controlling the flow of information.

Conversations in the form of interviews gave the interpreters a voice to talk about themselves and their own roles. The interviews expanded the statements they gave in the IPRI and their perceptions about themselves and about others. The interviews captured their stories, their anecdotes, and their fears, and allowed them to explain the reasons behind their "expanded or summarized renditions" (Wadensjö 1998). They also talked about the others with whom they interact. Some interpreters saw the patients' lack of education as problematic. Others saw the lack of exposure of healthcare providers to the social reality of patients as even more problematic. Some even referred to the social class of interpreters as being an obstacle to relating with patients. All of the interpreters at CH were aware of how they tailored their renditions to the social background of both patients and doctors. Some interpreters saw themselves as detectives, explorers, miners, and bridges. The fact that interpreters perceive themselves as visible and that they enact their visibility has several implications both at the theoretical and at the pragmatic level.

Theoretical implications

Studies from cognitive psychology have looked at interpreting as a highly sophisticated case of information processing and have mostly focused on conference interpreting. They have unveiled the complexities underlying the decoding and encoding processes, but they have isolated the act of interpreting from the interaction in which it is embedded. This caused a fragmentation in theory. Interpreting was regarded as only a cognitive act. In the last decade, studies crossing over from sociolinguistics have shifted this paradigm by shedding light on the interpreter as a co-participant. This research appears to separate itself from cognitive psychology rather than being in dialogue with it, and this contributes to an even deeper fragmentation in theory.

A theory of interpreting should integrate all of the complexities of this communicative act and should look at the act of interpreting in its entirety in context. External pressures which derive from the nature of the situation or occasion where interpreting occurs have also been somewhat overlooked. Examples of those pressures are those that come about by virtue of professional preparation (or lack thereof) of the interpreters and of the healthcare providers. Interpreters vary in their degree of training received, from none or on-the job training, to a Master's degree in translation and interpreting. HCPs are not necessarily trained in cross-cultural communication or in communicating through an interpreter. An integrative theory of interpreting should account for the differences in education of the interlocutors and the ways in which participants attempt to bridge those differences.

Other pressures also come about by the degree of prescriptiveness of the situation or occasion that requires interpreting, as well as the social constraints of the interaction. This means that it is essential to separate medical, community, court, and conference interpreting and consider the different pressures inherent in interactions in each of these settings. For instance, the courtroom interpreting process is strictly regulated. Turn-taking is not optional, and addressing interlocutors is also regulated. That is not the case with medical interpreting. Rules and regulations of the various settings exert different pressures on the interaction, an issue that must be addressed by a theory of interpreting. Additionally, if communicative functions (such as asking questions) are contextualized by setting, then it should be apparent that questions in a medical setting serve a very different purpose than questions in the courtroom. In the former, they are exploratory in nature; in the latter, parties ask questions assuming expected answers. The nature and the goals of the communicative functions constrain interpreting. This is an important point that should not be overlooked by a theory of interpreting.

Finally, it is important to differentiate between the public and private nature of the situations where interpreting takes place. For example, court and conference interpreting are public in nature. There is an audience, and interpreters are aware of that. They may act out their neutrality to meet the audience's expectations, to observe the codes of ethics, for the sake of their professional credibility or, as Wadensjö (1998) suggests, to pay lip service to the codes of the professional associations. There is no audience in an interpreted doctor–patient interview. The nature of that interaction is private. Public and private settings also impose different communicative rules on interpreters. The role of the interpreter may vary accordingly, and an encompassing theory needs to account for this variation.

A more integrative theory of interpreting, then, should account for the information-processing aspect of the task of the interpreter, together with the discursive interaction and the social context in which that interaction is embedded. It should also consider the three (or more) parties to the interaction, as they relate to each other as co-participants in an interpersonal relation. It would look at this interaction as embedded in an institution which is itself embedded in society at large. Thus, it would also consider the nature of the interaction (private or public) and the rules of communication that govern such interaction, as well as its communicative goals. Rather than prescribing how the role of an interpreter during an interaction should be, according to some ideal model, this new theory would describe the interpreter's role, based on situated practices of the parties at work. It would also consider the interpreter as a visible powerful individual who has agency in the interaction.

An encompassing theory of interpreting would consider cross-cultural and cross-linguistic communication in its broadest sense, and at all levels of society. It would also account for the education of interpreters and the developmental stages that an interpreter goes through to achieve proficiency. It would address issues in assessing and measuring interpreting skills, expanding the current focus – which is on the processing of information and the mastery of languages – to all the issues that encompass the act of interpreting, because interpreting is a social and political act.

Medical interpreters are sometimes members of an institution trying to channel services to the disenfranchised or to gate-keep the disenfranchised out of the system. They are members of a society that facilitates communication between speakers of majority and minority languages. In achieving such communication, interpreters are key players; they are not isolated from the other interlocutors. Isolating interpreters from the communicative circuit will not help the development of an encompassing theory of interpreting or cross-cultural communication. Cross-cultural and cross-linguistic communication needs to be considered as a whole if we want a genuine theory to emerge.

Practical implications

Cross-cultural and cross-linguistic communication in a medical setting   Communication between doctor and patient is more successful when characterized as informative, facilitative, responsive, and participatory (chapter 2). Many researchers have turned their attention to the interactions that occur during a medical interview (e.g. how physicians elicit information from patients and make information available and understandable to them). When this interaction occurs cross-linguistically and is facilitated by an interpreter, the doctor–patient relationship is affected in ways we have not yet explored. A general belief, however, is that the presence of the interpreter irons out differences between the parties and facilitates interactions, regardless of the interpreter's qualifications. Ingrained in the field of interpreting is the belief that the presence of the interpreter may not have an impact on outcomes, because the interpreter is invisible. Data from the present study not only show that the role of the interpreter has an impact on the doctor–patient interview in various ways, but also that interpreters are aware of that impact (although they only seem to view it in a positive light).

Observations of interpreted encounters and interviews with interpreters also allow us to explore the relationship between interpreters and healthcare providers. When healthcare providers request a particular interpreter and identify themselves, it is not unusual to hear a greeting from the interpreter if it is a provider with whom they frequently work (e.g. Elda: "Ah, doctor Chen, how are you doing this morning?"). The same holds true for patients with whom interpreters are already familiar. Interpreters usually greets patients by name and ask how they are doing (e.g. chapter 6, segment 2). When asked about their role, some interpreters said that they consider themselves a part of the healthcare team, and as such, they believe they help the provider deliver adequate healthcare. The fact that they consider themselves to be a part of the team may explain why they sometimes align themselves with the institution when they introduce themselves to patients (e.g. Mariana, chapter 6, segment 3: "I am an interpreter in this hospital, and I am going to help you so that you can communicate with Dr. Pang"). This feeling of partnership is not shared by all interpreters. For example, when Joaquín talks about his co-workers and his relationship to healthcare providers, he does not see himself as an equal partner with them, nor does he see himself as part of a team. He sees providers as enjoying higher status (chapter 7, Joaquín) and interpreters just being there to serve the communicative needs of the medical encounter. For other interpreters, like Consuelo, being singled out by a provider or being part of the team is not necessarily a positive thing. She feels ill at ease when providers request her instead of one of her fellow interpreters. For Consuelo, being requested represents more of a burden than an honor. She does not want to make the job personal, and she does not like feeling as though the provider depends on her specifically. She believes that providers and patients should not be permitted to request a specific interpreter, because that would imply a bond or an attachment that is, from her perspective, undesirable.

In a multicultural environment such as the one in which we live today, there is a high likelihood of two interlocutors not sharing a common language. Institutions that offer services to a diverse population must be aware of interpreting as a communicative need, and they should supply it. This also has implications for the education of healthcare providers.

Education of healthcare providers   Education of HCPs should emphasize the fact that patients coming from a different cultural/linguistic background do not automatically pose a problem. Since many HCPs exercise their profession in a multicultural environment, it is important that their education include some exposure to cross-cultural communication through interpreters. That way, when a situation arises in which a medical interpreter is present, the HCP can gain the full benefit of the interpreter's services. Through interpreters, HCPs may, for example, explore the differences in belief systems and in cultural norms. Many of the routinely used components of the medical culture, such as the pain scale, are not necessarily shared across cultures. Learning to relate to a patient through an interpreter in order to obtain information and build rapport is another way in which the provider can form a trusting relationship with the patient. In many cultures, the breaking of bad news in a direct manner is considered inappropriate and could render the HCP out of the patient's favor. This situation could be avoided by making the education of HCPs more inclusive of other cultural viewpoints and frames. Another important feature of HCP education about interpreters is that when they facilitate communication, providers must be aware that they may no longer be in complete control of what is said during the medical encounter.

In an increasingly multicultural society such as the United States, HCPs are communicating more and more frequently through interpreters. In addition to cultural diversity, the education of healthcare providers should include aspects of speaking with, to, and through an interpreter. Providers must realize that when they seek information about a patient's diet and merely tell the interpreter to ask the patient "about her diet," they no longer control the line of questioning that will follow (the HCP, in essence, allows the interpreter decide what to explore and what to ignore). This puts a tremendous amount of responsibility on the interpreter. If HCPs asked the questions in a more specific manner, interpreters would interpret those questions, and providers would remain in control of the exact information they wanted to elicit from patients. In other words, interpreters could bridge cultural gaps while HCPs retained control of their own responsibilities. This would not only allow HCPs to guide the encounter, but it would also limit the burden placed on medical interpreters, which would result in the best possible communicative process for patients.

In chapter 2, we discussed the impact that the presence of an interpreter in the medical encounter might have on the patient–provider relationship. In chapter 6 we explored different degrees of interpreters' visibility and how an increase in visibility can affect the personal and technical information conveyed and thus the relationship established during the encounter. Although this impact may sometimes be considered natural, given the fact that interpreters are after all co-participants in the interactions and therefore co-interlocutors, it does not come without consequences. As is evident from the data presented in chapter 6, very little is known about the consequences of interpreters' interventions. For example, what happens when an interpreter temporarily takes up the role of either the provider or the patient? What does it mean for an interpreter who has received no medical training to incur the responsibility of addressing medical issues? What does it mean for a healthcare provider to lose his/her voice and be temporarily replaced by an interpreter? This leads us right back to the question: who is in control and who remains in control of the interpreted medical encounter? In other words, who decides what information is relevant or crucial for the medical encounter and what information can be filtered out – the HCP or the interpreter? If interpreters edit patients' talk and decide which information is relevant to the medical issue at hand, then it is the interpreters who are making these important decisions. And on what basis? Their own opinions and experiences? Scientific knowledge? As we saw in chapter 6, interpreters are not solely responsible for this, since many times HCPs pass the floor (and the authority) to the interpreters by saying "ask him about chronic illnesses and all that" instead of exploring the chronic illnesses themselves at the necessary level of detail. This delegation of power, though, might also be viewed as a sign of the trust or confidence that HCPs have in the interpreters with whom they work daily. It is this feeling of being on equal ground with the HCPs that seems to make the interpreters feel that they are part of the healthcare team. By accepting too much responsibility for dialogue in the medical encounter, interpreters run the risk of inadvertently misleading patients, which can have counterproductive consequences. In other words, interpreters may unwittingly widen the gap between HCP and patients instead of bridging it.

Undoubtedly, interpreted discourse takes up more time than monolingual discourse. Although in the presence of linguistically diverse patients the use of an interpreter is the only way in which HCP and patients can communicate, the lengthening of the duration of the medical encounter, due to the presence of an interpreter, may be perceived as a drawback by some hospital administrators who are concerned about time. The presence of an interpreter may also be a double-edged sword for a patient who, on the one hand, relies on the presence of the interpreter to be able to communicate with the patient, but on the other hand feels at times bullied or patronized by the interpreter, despite the good intentions that interpreters may have.

The impact of an interpreter's presence on the medical encounter and the patient–provider relationship can be either positive or negative. In order to take full advantage of the services that the interpreter has to offer, healthcare providers should be trained in cross-cultural issues in the healthcare environment, as well as in the use of interpreters. Education in the use of medical interpreters can not only serve to shorten the duration of the interpreted medical encounter, but it may also help to minimize the frequency of misunderstandings that may occur in this setting.

The education and certification of interpreters   The opportunities for interpreting training in the US have been mostly for conference and court interpreters or introductory courses for translation/interpreting in general. There are programs at the BA level (e.g. the California State University at Los Angeles) or MA level (e.g. the Monterey Institute of International Studies offering a specialization in conference interpreting or a certificate on court interpreting). There are also shorter programs, such as certificates or workshops on a specific topic (e.g. insurance) or terminology (e.g. medical), which are offered by private companies that deliver telephonic interpreting (e.g. Language Line Services). Unlike other types of interpreting (e.g. conference or court) which have had a longer history of educational opportunities, medical interpreting training is in an emerging state. Some schools (e.g. New York University, the Monterey Institute of International Studies, and the University of Massachusetts at Amherst) have started on-line educational initiatives, which offer interpreters the opportunity to take a certain number of hours of instruction from home. The curriculum includes medical terminology, standards of practice, and protocols. Some face-to-face training of interpreting is also offered in the consecutive mode. Professional associations like the California Healthcare Interpreters Association (CHIA) offer workshops on ethics for medical interpreters and educational programs on how to implement the CHIA standards of practice and ethical principles.

The intricacies of medical interpreting often get lost in the shuffle during discussions about interpreting in general. Included among these intricacies is the dialogic (Wadensjö 1998) nature of the encounter, which implies that interpreters work equally for both speakers who are engaged in dialogue, into and out of their native language. Other unique features of the medical encounter include the co-construction of meaning and the power differential between the participants (Angelelli 2003a). Both of these features require that interpreters be aware that meaning does not exist in isolation from speakers and that not all speakers enjoy the same status when it comes to getting and keeping the floor. Another special characteristic of the medical encounter is that the interpreter may be required to address speakers that belong to different discourse communities (Hymes 1974, Angelelli 2000). This means that interpreters not only have to switch languages as they address the two interlocutors (HCP and patient), but they must also consider differences in registers and levels of education. In sum, the features that set medical interpreting apart from interpreting in other settings seldom get addressed and are often overshadowed during discussions about interpreting by some of the more general interpreting skills (e.g. memory or note-taking).

Currently, the institutions devoted to the education of interpreters in the US do not focus as much on the education of the individuals who facilitate communication across cultures as they do on the training of how to interpret. Whether in a Master's, Bachelor's, or a certificate program, the courses offered are of a pragmatic nature. The focus is not on educating well-rounded interpreters as much as it is on training in specific areas, such as information-processing skills or terminology. Education is confused with training.

Courses on cross-cultural communication, interpersonal relations, or social psychology would expose students of interpreting to the types of interactions in which they will eventually be participating (contextualization of interpreting). Courses in sociolinguistics and discourse analysis would empower students to problematize meaning and how it gets co-constructed by the parties. Problematizing the co-construction of meaning, rather than teaching students that there is only one meaning which is automatically constructed, would not only groom students to be more analytical and critical, but it would also raise awareness about the crucial role played by interpreters in this construction. Courses in dialectology, varieties of language, and language register would help students contextualize language use and language users. Courses on issues specific to the settings in which interpreters work (e.g. power imbalance, institutional cultures, protocol, or ethics) would enhance student preparation. This integral education would also affect how student interpreters are assessed and certified.

Currently, the interpreter certification process measures interpreters' ability to interpret consecutively and simultaneously. It also tests memory and terminology in both languages for which the interpreter is seeking certification. The underlying assumption is that the only skills that are worth testing are linguistic and information processing. Certification procedures should not overlook the fact that interpreting is an interaction (Wadensjö 1998), as well as a discourse process (Roy 2000). The interpersonal role of the interpreter needs to be integrated in the assessment of interpreters. Issues of alignment, affect, trust, and respect should be present in the certification and assessment of interpreters, rather than simply ignored (Angelelli 2003). This broader view of assessment would result in professionals who are better prepared to serve the communicative needs of individuals at all levels of society.

The professional organizations   A thorough understanding of the interpersonal role of the interpreter may allow professional associations to better serve their members and, consequently, the members of the less dominant cultures for whom interpreters work. Rather than theoretically prescribing what the role of the interpreter should be, associations could encourage and fund research to explore and understand the role of the interpreter in each of the different settings where interpreters work. The pressures and constraints that result from each of the different settings should be considered from the perspective of the three interlocutors. More studies are needed that both address the interactive and interpersonal challenges of interpreting and acknowledge the power that the interpreter holds, as well as how this power plays itself out in the different settings where interpreters work.

At the time this study was conducted, California Hope was a pioneer in telephonic interpreting. Currently, several companies in the US offer telephonic interpreting among their services. This is an issue that is not even debated by the professional associations that regulate standards of practice. Proponents of telephonic interpreting base their arguments on productivity rates and practicality. Opponents argue that personal elements are lost during telephonic interpreting. This research shows that the interplay of social factors is present in every type of interpreted medical encounter, whether face-to-face or over the speakerphone. Further study is necessary in order to fully understand the impact of the interpreter's physical presence (or lack thereof) in the responsible co-construction of meaning during an ICE. Unfortunately, current prescriptivism does not allow the associations to address the complexity of the role of the interpreter as it unfolds fully in practice.

Concerns and curiosities revisited

This study of the role of interpreters at California Hope revealed that interpreters, in the interactions they broker, are visible co-participants who, triggered by the interplay of social factors, exercise their agency. In doing so, they cooperatively broker communication between speakers who do not have a common language, all the while conforming to the rules of the institution where they work.

Few things impact on our lives more than our ability to communicate. Today, in the multilingual and multicultural society in which we live, many people can only exercise their ability to communicate with the help of interpreters. Interpreters facilitate communication between speakers of majority and minority languages. Every communicative event involves power differentials. In the new paradigm that portrays the interpreter as a co-participant and co-constructor, the present study has shed light on the interpreters' agency manifested as visibility. Throughout this book, we have seen how visible interpreters play a significant role in brokering communication during interpreted communicative events. In those events, we have also seen how participants make assumptions and how their perceptions of reality color their interactions. We have seen that interactions do not occur in a social vacuum. In sum, we have seen how the myth of neutrality and invisibility cannot be maintained by social beings during interactions that occur in an institution which is part of the society where it exists.

All of the interpreted communicative events that we have seen at California Hope involved disenfranchised people. Visible interpreters facilitated all of these events. When conversations between the disenfranchised and the dominant take place, power differentials emerge. When those power differentials are overlooked or denied because interpreters are considered invisible, the status quo is perpetuated. Practitioners, professional associations, and educational institutions cannot be solely responsible for addressing this issue. Cross-cultural communication touches all of us. We, as a society, need to ask ourselves why we feel the need to continue labeling the interpreter as invisible and, equally importantly, why we believe interpreting to be immune to the effects of social factors. Addressing the visibility of the interpreter is an ideological imperative for the field. Breaking through the ideology of invisibility becomes a political imperative for all.

References

AIIC. 2002. *Annuaire 2002.* Geneva, Switzerland: AIIC.

Adler, H. 2002. The sociophysiology of caring in the doctor-patient relationship. *Journal of General Internal Medicine* 17: 874–81.

Allen, J. 2000. Worlds and words apart. *LA Times*, November 6, 2000. (Active November 6, 2000.) http://www.latimes.com/print/health/20001106/t000106263.html

Angelelli, C. V. 2000. Interpreting as a communicative event: a look through Hymes' lenses. *Meta (Journal des Traducteurs)* 45 (4): 580–92.

    2001. Deconstructing the invisible interpreter: a critical study of the interpersonal role of the interpreter in a cross-cultural/linguistic communicative event. PhD diss., Stanford University.

    2003. The interpersonal role of the interpreter in cross-cultural communication: a survey of conference, court, and medical interpreters in the US, Canada and Mexico. In *The Critical Link 3. Interpreters in the Community*, 15–26. John Benjamins: Amsterdam.

    2003a. The visible collaborator: interpreter intervention in doctor/patient encounters. In M. Metzger, ed. *From Topic Boundaries to Omission: New Research on Interpretation*. Washington, DC: Gallaudet University Press.

Baker, D., R. Hayes, and J. P. Fortier. 1998. Interpreter use and satisfaction with interpersonal aspects of care for Spanish-speaking patients. *Medical Care* 36 (10): 1461–70.

Barnett, S. 2002. Cross-cultural communication with patients who use American Sign Language. *Family Medicine* 34 (5): 376–82.

Becker, A. 1995. *Beyond Translation: Essays towards a Modern Philology.* Michigan: University of Michigan Press.

Berk-Seligson, S. 1990. *The Bilingual Courtroom: Court Interpreters in the Judicial Process.* Chicago: University of Chicago Press.

Bolden, G. 2000. Toward understanding practices of medical interpreting: interpreters' involvement in history taking. *Discourse Studies* 2 (4): 387–419.

Bourdieu, P. 1977. *Outline of a Theory of Practice*, 1st edn. Cambridge Studies in Social Anthropology 16. Cambridge: Cambridge University Press.

    1990. *In Other Words: Essays Towards a Reflexive Sociology.* Trans. Matthew Adamson. Stanford, CA: Stanford University Press.

    1991. *Language and Symbolic Power.* Cambridge, MA: Harvard University Press.

Brewer, M. B. 1988. A dual process model of impression formation. In J. Thomas K. Srull and Robert S. Wyer, eds. *Advances in Social Cognition*, vol. I: 1–36. Hillsdale, NJ: Lawrence Erlbaum.

Buber, M. 1970. *I and Thou.* Trans. Walter Kaufmann. New York: Charles Scribner's Sons.

Byrne, P. S. and B. E. I. Long. 1976. *Doctors Talking to Patients: a Study of the Verbal Behaviours of Doctors in Consultation.* London: HMSO.

Cambridge, J. 1999. Information loss in bilingual medical interviews through an untrained interpreter. *The Translator* 5 (2): 201–19.

Campbell, T. L., S. H. McDaniel, K. Cole-Kelly, J. Hepworth, and A. Lorenz. 2002. Family interviewing: a review of the literature in primary care. *Family Medicine* 34 (5): 312–18.

Candace, C. 1990. Emotions and micropolitics in everyday life. In T. D. Kemper, ed. *Research Agendas in the Sociology of Emotions*, 305–33. Albany: SUNY Press.

Candib, L. 1995. *Medicine and the Family: a Feminist Perspective.* New York: Basic-Books.

CHIA Standards and Certification Committee. 2002. *California Standards for Health-care Interpreters: Ethical Principles, Protocols, and Guidance on Roles & Intervention.* The California Endowment: California.

Davidson, B. 1998. Interpreting medical discourse: a study of cross-linguistic communication in the hospital clinic. PhD diss., Stanford University.

  2000. The interpreter as institutional gatekeeper: the social-linguistic role of interpreters in Spanish–English medical discourse. *Journal of Sociolinguistics* 4 (3): 379–405.

  2001. Questions in cross-linguistic medical encounters: the role of the hospital interpreter. *Anthropological Quarterly* 74 (4): 170–8.

Duranti, A. 1992. Intentions, self and responsibility: an essay in Samoan ethopragmatics. In Hill and Irvine 1992: 24–47.

Engel, G. L. 1988. How much longer must medicine's science be bound by a 17th-century world view? In White 1988.

Feagin, J. 1991. The continuing significance of race: anti-black discrimination in public places. *American Sociological Review* 56: 101–16.

Festinger, L. 1954. A theory of social comparison processes. *Human Relations* 7: 117–40.

Ferguson, W. J. and L. M. Candib. 2002. Culture, language, and the doctor-patient relationship. *Family Medicine* 34 (5): 353–61.

Fiske, S. T. and S. E. Taylor. 1991. *Elements of Social Cognition.* New York: McGraw Hill.

Flores, G. 2000. Culture and the patient-physician relationship: achieving cultural competency in healthcare. *Journal of Pediatrics* 136: 14–23.

Foschi, M. and E. Lawler, eds. 1994. *Group Processes: Sociological Analyses.* Chicago: Nelson-Hall.

Frey, J. 1998. The clinical philosophy of family medicine. *American Journal of Medicine* 104: 327–9.

García, A. 2000. Remote telephone interpreting system implemented at Santa Clara Valley Medical. *CHIA Newsletter* 2 (2): 1.

Ginsberg, C., V. A. Martin, Y. Shaw-Taylor, and C. McGregor. 1995. *Interpretation and Translation Services in Health Care: a Survey of US Public and Private Teaching Hospitals.* Washington, DC: National Public Health and Hospital Institute.

Goffman, E. 1981. *Forms of Talk.* Philadelphia: University of Pennsylvannia Press.

Heath, C. 1992. The delivery and reception of diagnosis in the general-practice consultation. In P. Drew and J. Heritage, eds. *Talk at Work*, 580. Cambridge: Cambridge University Press.

Hill, J. and J. Irvine, eds. 1992. *Responsibility and Evidence in Oral Discourse.* Cambridge Studies in the Social and Cultural Foundations of Language. Cambridge: Cambridge University Press.

Hill, J. and O. Zepeda, 1992. Mrs. Patricio's trouble: the distribution of responsibility in an account of personal experience. In Hill and Irvine 1992: 197–226.

Hochschild, A. 1983. *The Managed Heart: Commercialization of Human Feeling.* Berkeley: University of California Press.

Hornberger, J., C. Gibson, W. Wood, C. Degueldre, I. Corso, B. Palla, and D. Bloch. 1996. Eliminating language barriers for non-English-speaking patients. *Medical Care* 8: 845–56.

Hymes, D. 1974. *Foundations in Sociolinguistics.* New Jersey: University of Pennsylvania Press.

Irvine, J. 1992. Insult and responsibility: verbal abuse in a Wolof village. In Hill and Irvine 1992: 105–34.

Jacobs, E., D. Lauderdale, J. Meltzer, J. Shorey, W. Levinson, and R. Thisted. 2001. Impact of interpreter services on delivery of healthcare to limited-English-proficient patients. *Journal of General and Internal Medicine* 16: 468–74.

Kaufert, J. and R. Putsch. 1997. Communication through interpreters in healthcare: ethical dilemmas arising from differences in class, culture, language and power. *The Journal of Clinical Ethics* 8 (1): 71–87.

Kuo, D. and M. Fagan. 1999. Satisfaction with methods of Spanish interpretation in an ambulatory care clinic. *Journal of General and Internal Medicine* 14: 547–50.

LeCompte, M. and J. Schensul. 1999. *Analyzing and Interpreting Ethnographic Data.* Walnut Creek: Altamira.

Lee, S. J., A. L. Back, S. D. Block, and S. K. Stewart. 2002. Enhancing physician-patient communication. *Hematology* 1: 464–90.

Levy, E. 1999. A social-pragmatic account of the development of planned discourse. *Human Development* 42 (5): 225–47.

Marcus, E. 2003. When a patient is lost in the translation. *New York Times.* New York: F7.

Manson, A. 1988. Language concordance as a determinant of patient compliance and emergency room use in patients with asthma. *Medical Care* 26: 1119–28.

Marx, K. 1993. *Capital.* Provo, Utah: Regal Publications.

Massachusetts Medical Interpreters Association. 1995. *Medical Interpreting Standards of Practice.* Boston: Massachusetts Medical Interpreters Association.

Metzger, M. 1999. *Sign Language Interpreting: Deconstructing the Myth of Neutrality.* Washington, DC: Gallaudet University Press.

Miles, M. B. and A. M. Huberman. 1984. *Qualitative Data Analysis: a Sourcebook of New Methods.* Beverly Hills, CA: Sage.

NAJIT. 2003. *Code of Ethics and Professional Responsibilities.* http://www.najit.org/ethics.html

Niebhur, H. R. 1963. *The Responsible Self.* New York: Harper and Row.

Prince, C. 1986. Hablando con el doctor: communication problems between doctors and their Spanish-speaking patients. PhD diss., Stanford University.

Random House Webster's Dictionary. 1997. 1st edn. New York: Random House Publishers.

Reddy, M., ed. 1979. *The Conduit Metaphor: a Case of Frame Conflict in our Language about Language.* Cambridge: Cambridge University Press.

Ridgeway, C. 1993. Legitimacy, status and dominance in groups. In S. Worschel and J. Simpson, eds. *Conflict between People and Groups,* 110–27. Chicago: Nelson-Hall.

——— 1994. Affect. In Foschi and Lawler 1994: 205–30.

Rivadeneyra, R., V. Elderkin-Thompson, R. C. Silver, and H. Waitzkin. 2000. Patient centeredness in medical encounters requiring an interpreter. *American Journal of Medicine* 108: 470–4.

Rosenberg, E., M. Lussier, and M. Beaudoin. 1997. Lessons for clinicians from physician-patient communication literature. *Archives of Family Medicine* 6: 279–83.

Rosenhan, D. L. 1973. On being sane in insane places. *Science* 179: 250–8.

Roter, D. 2002. Three blind men and an elephant: reflections on meeting the challenges of patient diversity in primary care practice. *Family Medicine* 34 (5): 390–3.

Roy, C. 1989. A sociolinguistic analysis of the interpreter's role in the turn exchanges of an interpreted event. PhD diss., Georgetown University, Washington, DC.

——— 2000. *Interpreting as a Discourse Process.* New York and Oxford: Oxford University Press.

Sacther, S. and J. Singer. 1962. Cognitive, social and psychological determinants of emotional state. *Psychological Review* 69: 379–99.

Seleskovitch, D. and M. Lederer. 1989. *Pédagogie raisonnée de l'interprétation.* Brussels: Didier Erudition Opoce.

Shuy, R. 1976. The medical interview: problems in communication. *Primary Care* 3: 365–86.

Smith-Lovin, L. 1990. Emotion as the confirmation and disconfirmation of identity: an affect control model. In T. D. Kemper, ed. *Research Agendas in the Sociology of Emotions,* 238–70. Albany, NY: SUNY Press.

Stewart, M. A. 1995. Effective physician-patient communication and health outcomes: a review. *Canadian Medical Association Journal – Journal de l'Association médicale canadienne* 152 (9): 1423–33.

Stouffer, S. A., E. A. Suchman, L. C. DeVinney, C. A. Star, and R. M. Williams. 1949. *The American Soldier: Adjustment during Army Life,* vol. I. Princeton, NJ: Princeton University Press.

Tannen, D. 1984. *Conversational Style: Analyzing Talk among Friends.* Norwood, NJ: Ablex.

US Census. 2000. Language spoken at home and ability to speak English for the population 5 years and over by state: 2000.

Van Maanen, J. 1988. *Tales of the Field: on Writing Ethnography.* Chicago: University of Chicago Press.

Vygotsky, L. 1934 (Rpt. 1986). *Thought and Language.* Trans. Alex Kozulin. Cambridge, MA: MIT Press.

——— 1978. *Mind in Society: the Development of Higher Psychological Processes,* ed. M. Cole, V. S. Steiner, S. Scribner, and E. Souberman. Cambridge, MA: Harvard University Press.

Wadensjö, C. 1992. Interpreting as interaction: on dialogue-interpreting in immigration hearings and medical encounters. PhD diss., Linköping University: Linköping Studies in Arts and Science.

1995. Dialogue interpreting and the distribution of responsibility. *Hermes, Journal of Linguistics* 14: 111–29.

1998. *Interpreting as Interaction.* New York: Addison Wesley Longman Inc.

Weber, W. 1984. *Training Translators and Conference Interpreters.* New York: Harcourt Brace Jovanovich, Inc.

Webster, M. and M. Foschi, eds. 1998. *Status Generalization: New Theory and Research.* Stanford: Stanford University Press.

White, K. 1988. *The Task of Medicine: Dialogue at Wickenburg.* Menlo Park, CA: The Henry Kaiser Foundation.

Wittgenstein, L. 1931/1980. *Culture and Value.* Trans. Peter Winch, ed. G. H. von Wright. Oxford: Basil Blackwell.

Wong, D. and D. Shen. 1999. Factors influencing the process of translating. *Meta* 44 (1): 78–100.

Yee, L., M. Diaz, and T. Spitzer. 2003. California Assembly Bill 292. Info.sen.ca.gov/pub/bill/ASM/ab_0251_0300/ab_292_bill_20030206_introduced.html

Zoppi, K., and R. M. Epstein. 2002. Is communication a skill? Communication behaviors and being in relation. *Family Medicine* 34 (5): 319–24.

Index

abrupt 120, 121
access 1, 2, 3, 7, 11, 19, 20, 130
  to healthcare 21, 22
accessible 118
accuracy 7, 30, 106, 122
accurate(ly) 109, 122
ad hoc interpreter 2, 22
adjustment 126
Adler, H. 15, 16
advocate 11
affect 11, 84
affect-control theory 27
age 9, 19, 49, 50
agency of interpreters 3, 9, 10, 26, 28, 29, 32,
    41, 42, 67, 76, 86, 87, 89, 132, 134, 140,
    141
aid 125
align 7, 11, 12, 121, 123
alignment 115, 124
Allen, J. 1
American Sign Language (ASL) 8, 13
Angelelli, C. V. xi, 11, 16, 139
  co-construction of meaning 139
  power differential in the medical
    encounter 139
answer
  specific 129
  yes or no 88, 126
answering questions 112, 120, 123
arbitrator 123
asking questions 120, 134
attach 112
attribution theory 27, 31
audience 134

bad news 19, 119, 121, 126, 136
Baker, D. 22, 23, 24
balance(d) 11, 124
Barnett, S. 22
Becker, A. L. 73, 103, 104
  contextual interpretation of text 103

beliefs 5, 10, 28, 136
  folk 125
Berk-Seligson, S. 4, 8, 9, 10, 73, 75
biases 31–2
bilingual social worker 124
body language 123, 124
Bolden, G. 12
bond 108, 121, 136
Bourdieu P. 26, 27, 28, 97, 102, 128
  theory of practice 26, 27, 28
Brewer, M. B. 11, 27, 29, 30, 80, 83, 85, 89,
    94, 127
  impression formation theory 27, 29, 30,
    127
  system of categories 85, 94
bridges 3, 22, 67, 133
brokering
  a term 122, 124, 125
  of comprehension 89, 91, 97, 127
Buber, M. 15
  I and Thou 15

California Healthcare Interpreters Association
  (CHIA) 1, 23, 138
California Standards for Healthcare
  Interpreters 23
California Hope xi, 2, 3, 4, 5, 44, 46
Cambridge, J. 1, 12
Campbell, T. L. 22
Candace, C. 27
  affect-control theory 27
Candib, L. 15, 16, 19, 20, 21, 22, 24
  empathic bond between doctor and
    patient 16
  Medicine and the Family 124
category 29
  category resistance 30
certification 1
Civil Rights Act of 1964 1
clarification 120
clarifier 126

class 4, 13, 28, 29, 118, 133
class differences 110
co-constructor 141
code of ethics 1, 2, 13, 134
cognitive psychology 133
complex 3, 9, 10, 14, 19, 102, 124
complexity 21, 112, 133, 140
compliance 20, 125
complicated 124
comply 124, 125, 126
communication
    conduit model 7
    cross-cultural 1
    cross-linguistic 1
conference interpreter 138
consent 13, 20, 44, 45, 63, 67, 88, 89
construct meaning 128
co-construction of meaning 7, 14, 41, 132,
        139, 140
co-participant 133, 134
Conte, CA 46
control traffic of information 137
corner the patient 120
court interpreter 138
create text 127
cultural
    background 15, 17, 29
    beliefs 19
    broker 13, 127
    differences 19, 25, 112, 115
    gap 11, 137
    Mexican-medical 122
    norms (blueprints) 10, 85, 132,
        136
    values 19
culture 4, 13

data 5
    analysis 5
    artifacts 5, 59
    audio recordings 5, 45
    coding 5
    collection, coding 58, 59
    field notes 5, 59–61
    interviews 5, 62–3
    IPRI 61
    recordings of ICEs 63–4
    questionnaires 5
    sources 132
Davidson, B. 3, 7, 8, 9, 10, 11, 12, 26, 67
    interpreters as gatekeepers 7, 12
deliver news or results 123
detach 112
detective 129, 133
diamond connoisseurs 131

dilemma 2, 3, 13
discourse
    analysis 41, 139
    medical 12, 18
disparities 20
disposition 27
distance 23
distinct 123
diverse 125
doctor/physician–patient relationship 15, 16,
        19, 20, 22, 23, 88, 89, 137
    biopsychosocial paradigm 16, 17, 18
dominant
    less 7
    more 7
Duranti, A. 27, 41, 94, 99, 128

educate 121, 122, 125, 126, 130
education 4, 94, 106, 120, 125, 133, 134, 139
    of healthcare providers 136–7, 138
    of interpreters 138–40
    level of 120, 123, 127, 130, 133
    of patients 113, 114
    problematic 127
effect-dependent 29
enabler 126
Engel, G. L. 16
Epstein, R. M. 15, 16
ethical principles 2
ethics 138, 139
    code of 1, 2, 13, 134
ethnicity 9, 10, 17, 20
ethnography of communication xi, 4, 41, 44
ethnographic approach 4, 11, 13, 132
expand 109, 127
experience 122
explain 109, 121
explanation 13
explore 122
explorer 133

face-to-face 5, 48, 123, 138, 140
Fagan, M. 20, 22, 23
family members 23
Feagin, J. 27, 30
    impression formation 27
fear 114, 116–17, 133
    of being sued 122
Ferguson, W. J. 16, 19, 20, 21, 22, 24
Festinger, L. 11, 27, 30, 81, 97, 102
    social comparison theory 27, 30, 96, 97
fieldwork 58
Fiske, S. T. 27, 31, 94
    attribution theory 27, 31; biases and
        errors 31–2

Flores, G. 19, 20, 21, 22
folk beliefs 125
Foschi, M. 27, 32, 88
    status characterization theory 27, 32, 88
footing 13
fragmentation of theory of interpreting
    133
frame theory 13
framework 9
Frey, J. 16

gap 124
García, A. 22
gender 9, 10, 17
giving advice 124
Goffman, E. 76
    concept of footing 13
    framework 9

habitus 27, 28, 29, 97, 102
Hablamos Juntos 1
healthcare access 21, 22
healthcare providers' education 136–7, 138
Heath, C. 75
help 125, 135
helper 127
hierarchy 116–17
Hill, J. 27, 40, 41, 42
Hochschild, A. 27
    affect-control theory 27
Hornberger, J. 19, 21
Huberman, A. M. 58
Hymes, D. 8, 10, 27, 33, 97, 99, 102, 139
    differences between MCE and ICE 34–40
    speech community 33, 97, 99, 102, 139
    taxonomy of speaking 33–4, 85

ignore 11
illiterate 121
impact 135, 137, 138
index 66–7
information
    dependent 29
    extract 131
    loss of 124
    pass along 124
    prioritize 120
    processing 133, 134, 140
    readily available 131
    relevant 120
    request of 131
    right 120
    valuable 125
initiative 89, 93
    take 89, 127

institution 4, 10, 27, 28, 29, 76, 77, 85, 88,
    134, 135, 136, 141
insulting 123
interaction 15, 16, 114, 119, 133, 135,
    139
interdisciplinary xi
    lens 132
interviews 127, 132
integrative theory of interpreting 134–5
interlocutors, distribution of responsibility
    13
interpersonal relations 26, 28, 134, 139
interpersonal role of interpreters 67
interpreted communicative event (ICE) 8
    closings 76, 77, 82–5
    intention of 70–1
    nature of 69–70, 73–4
    openings 76, 79–82
    phases of 75
interpreters
    ad hoc 2, 22
    advocates 13, 114
    agency 3, 9, 10, 26, 28, 29, 32, 41, 42, 67,
        76, 86, 87, 89, 134, 140, 141
    bridge between cultures, languages 118,
        120
    brokers 40, 109–14, 140, 141
    camaraderie 51
    certification 1
    channel 14, 135
    co-constructors 8, 11, 41, 42, 67
    co-conversationalists 12
    co-interlocutors 82
    co-owners 79
    co-participants 8–9, 11, 14, 26, 67, 75, 140,
        141
    conference 138
    court 138
    creators of text 76, 99
    detectives 129
    distribution of responsibility 42
    education, certification 138–40
    educators 40
    explorers 133
    facilitators 114
    filters 114–17, 120
    gatekeepers 7, 12, 34
    helpers 127
    invisibility 3, 141
    invisible 8, 32, 135, 141
    invisible language facilitators 7
    invisible mechanical language experts 132
    language conduits 26, 75
    language intermediaries 13
    members of speech communities 10

interpreters (*cont.*)
  metaphors 5, 129; bridges 136;
    detectives 129; diamond
    connoisseurs 131; mine-diggers 125;
    miners 131
  neutral 32
  owners of text 77, 84, 85–102
  perception of role 105
  powerful parties 3, 9, 134
  prescribed role 26
  prescribed vs. actual role 2, 107, 129
  register scale 97
  related distortion 12–13
  responsibility 14, 18, 40, 41, 99, 102, 107,
    109, 120, 128, 129, 131, 137
  role 4, 5
  role across settings 74
  social responsibility 42
  speech tailoring 89
  summarizers 40
  traffic controllers 40
  training 133, 138
  untrained 22
  visibility 9–10, 14, 76, 130, 132; degrees
    of 45; major 85, 102; minor 102;
    overview 75–6; subcategories 69
  visible 10, 14, 134, 140
  visible co-participants with agency
    132
interpreter interpersonal role inventory
    (IPRI) 59, 61
interpreting
  ad hoc 22; advantages 23;
    disadvantages 23
  as a discourse process 140
  as an interaction 140
  benefits of interpreting services 24
  community 133
  conference 133
  court 133, 138
  medical 133, 134, 138, 139
  medical, evolution of 1–2
  negative aspects of interpreting services
    24
  negative consequences of not having
    interpreting services 25
  standardization 23
  telephone 48, 140
Interpreting Services (IS) at California Hope
    (CH) 44, 48
  layout 53
  manager 45, 48, 49, 105
  requirements for employment 49
  staff 48, 49; Annette 108; Consuelo 110;
    Elda 112; Joaquín 114; Julio 118;

  Marcos 120; Mariana 121; Mauro 123;
    Rogelio 124; Roberto 105; Vicente 125
interviews 12, 105, 128
intonation 123
invisible 2, 8, 14, 32, 135, 141
invisibility 2–3, 141
  challenging the notion 3
  concept 8
  model 7
  myth of 2–3
Irvine, J. 27, 40, 41, 74, 92

Jacobs, E. 15, 19, 20, 21, 22, 23, 24,
    25

Kaufert, J. 12, 13, 14, 18, 24
kind 124
knowledge 121
Kuo, D. 20, 22, 23

language
  barrier 19, 21
  differences 19
  switcher 14
LeCompte, M. 58
lecturing 122
Lederer, M. (Figure 1) 8
Lee, S. J. 15, 19, 20
lenses (for viewing interpreter's role)
  interplay of lenses 42–3
  linguistic anthropology 26, 27, 33, 40, 41,
    99
  social theory 26, 29, 32
  sociological theory 26, 29, 32
level of education 120, 123, 127, 130,
    133
Levy, E.
life-learning 122
limitation 122
limited-English
  proficiency 18
  speaking 1, 2, 25
line of questioning 88, 129, 137
linguistic anthropology 26
link 124
log 55, 120
loss of information 124
loud voice 121

majority languages 135
make diagnosis 121
Manson, A. 20
Marcus, E. 1, 20
Marx, K. 7, 14
  Capital 7

Massachusetts Medical Interpreters
    Association (MMIA) 1, 23
meaning 7, 29, 128
    co-construction 7, 14, 41
    social construction 41
mediate 123
mediation 13
medical encounter
    dialogic nature 139
    patient-centered 17
    relationship-centered 17, 89, 91, 99;
        facilitative 17, 87, 102, 135;
        informative 87, 91, 102, 135; medically
        functional 17; participatory 18, 87, 91,
        135; responsive 8, 87, 102, 135
medicalese 110
metaphors 129; *see under* interpreters
Metzger, M. 2, 3, 8, 9, 11, 12, 13, 75
Miles, M. B. 58
mine-diggers 125
miners 131, 133
minority
    languages xii, 135; speakers of 3
    physicians 20
    patients 20, 21
myth 2

NAJIT 74
nationality 9
navigate 124
    cultural perspectives 130
needs 122
negotiate 13
neutral 2, 26, 120, 121
neutrality 3, 13, 134
    challenging the notion 8
non-compliance 102, 120, 125
non-English-speaking patients 21, 24

objectivity 124
offensive 124
opaque 10, 11
orchestrate 127
order 121
ownership 76, 127

pain (rating) scale 97, 98, 99, 109, 112, 120,
        122, 123, 126, 127, 136
pas de trois 25
patient-centered approach 17
patient-centered encounters 16
patient compliance 22
patient, limited-English speaking 1, 20
patronize 121, 122
pave the way 126

perception 61, 133, 141
pilot study 44
planned talk 74
power 9, 10, 13, 28, 30, 31, 32, 88, 94, 121,
        137, 139, 140
power differential 121, 141
powerful 3, 9, 134
precise 122
pressed for time 118, 125, 126, 130
pressure 111, 133, 134, 140
preventive medicine 125
Prince, C. 10, 12
problematic 2, 133
professional association 2, 3, 134, 138, 140
protect 121
protection 121
Putsch R. 12, 13, 14, 18, 24

race 9, 10, 20
rapport 18, 21, 114, 118, 124, 130, 136
reciprocity 12
Reddy, M. 7
    conduit model of communication 7
regionalism 121
register 11, 96, 97, 113, 120, 127, 139
    scale 11
relationship 4, 25, 27–8, 127
    caring 16
    centered medicine 17
    collaborative 16
    definition 15
    discordant 16
    vs. interaction 15
    doctor/physician–patient, *see*
        doctor/physician–patient relationship
    participatory 18, 87, 91, 135
    patient-centered 20
renditions 109
    expanded 17
    summarized 17
reprimand 121
respect 11, 122, 126
responsibility 14, 18, 40, 41, 99, 102, 107,
        109, 112, 120, 128, 129, 131, 137
    achieved cooperatively 41
    contextually and cooperatively defined 41,
        128
    owned 41
responsible 121, 141
    role 18
    socially 40
repetition 120
Ridgeway, C. 27, 32
    affect-control theory 27
Rivadeneyra, R. 20, 21, 24

Robert Wood Johnson Foundation 1
  Hablamos Juntos 1
role of interpreters 26; *see also* interpreters
  actual 129
  concept of visibility 9–10, 11
  co-participant with agency
  different forms 7
  Goffman's framework 9
  invisible 129
  prescribed 129
  prescribed vs. actual 2
  visible 9, 11, 129
Rosenberg, E. 15
Rosenhan, D. L. 27, 30
  impression formation 27
Roter, D. 17, 18, 19
Roy, C. 3, 8, 9, 10, 11, 67, 74, 75, 140
rude 111, 122
rush 125

Sacther, S. 27
  affect-control theory 27
sad news 128
scale 97, 98, 99, 109, 120, 122, 123, 125, 126,
  127, 136
Schensul, J. 58
self (the) 10, 29, 30
Seleskovitch, D. (Figure 1) 8
seniority 122
sensitive 123
setting 134, 140
  public vs. private 74, 134
shame 121
Shuy, R. 12, 13
significant other (theory of) 27, 30
Singer, J. 27
  affect-control theory 27
site 44
Smith-Lovin, L. 27
  affect-control theory 27
situated practices 134
social baggage 26, 128
social construction of meaning 41
social context 134
social differences 108, 115–18
social factors 4, 9, 10, 11, 26, 29, 76, 77, 92,
  99, 102, 127, 140, 141
social interaction xi
socially oriented peers 102
social reality 127, 133
social theory 4, 26
  psychology 4, 10, 139
social understanding 111
social vacuum 8, 9, 26, 28, 76, 141
societal blueprints 132

society 4, 9, 10, 27, 29, 76, 77, 134, 135, 141
socio-economic status (SES) 9, 125
sociological theory 26
soften 121
solidarity 9, 10, 80, 83, 84, 92, 94
speakerphone 5, 22, 48, 123, 140
specific answers 129
speech community 33, 97, 99, 102, 139
spontaneous talk 74
Statistical Package for the Social Sciences
  (SPSS) 61
standards of practice 2, 23, 138, 140
status 9, 30, 31, 32, 136, 139
status characterization theory 27, 32
story 120, 130, 131, 133
  telling a 110, 113, 115, 126
Stouffer, S. A. 11, 30
summarize 114, 127
sued, fear of being 122

tailor 110, 127, 133
take initiative 89, 127
talk 74
  co-constructing 8
  construction of 8, 99
  facilitating 8
  planned vs. spontaneous 74
  repairing 8
taxonomy of speaking 33–4, 85
Taylor, S. E. 27, 31, 94
  attribution theory 27, 31; biases and
    errors 31–2
team player 122, 135–6
teamwork 13
technical terms 109, 121
tension 110, 128, 129
testing 139–40
text
  create a 76, 127
  ownership 76, 127
theory of affect-control 27
theory of attribution 27, 31
theory of impression formation 27, 29, 30,
  127
theory of practice 26, 27, 28
theory of the significant other 27, 30
theory of social comparison 27, 30, 96, 97
theory of status characterization 27, 32,
  88
threats 126
tone down 123, 124
tone of voice 109, 113–14, 116, 120, 123
traffic flow 11
training 133, 138
translation 56

transparent 10, 11
treatment
  of illness 125
  of person 125
trust 11, 22, 23, 24, 45, 89, 109, 122, 124,
  125, 130, 137
turn-taking 134

uniform 123
US Census 18

Van Maanen, J. 105
visibility of interpreters 9–10, 14, 76, 130,
  132
  degrees of 45
  major 85, 102
  minor 102
  overview 75–6
  subcategories 69
visible model of interpreter 11
visible role of interpreters, *see* interpreters
voice 109, 123, 124, 132, 137
  tone of 123
  volume 123

Vygotsky, L. 44, 57, 72
  Mind in Society 44

Wadensjö, C. 3, 8, 9, 10, 11, 12, 13, 14, 25,
  67, 74, 75, 83, 86–102, 109, 133, 134,
  139, 140
  closed renditions 86–102
  communicative *pas de trois* 25
  dialogic nature of medical encounter 139
  expanded renditions 83, 88, 94, 97, 99, 127,
    133
  taxonomy of utterances 75
water down 55, 120, 121, 128
Webster, M. 27, 32, 88
  status characterization theory 27, 32, 88
White, K.
Wittgenstein, L. 26, 42
  Culture and Value 26

Yee, L. 1
yes or no answer 88, 126

Zepeda, O. 27, 42
Zoppi, K. 15, 16